Dee. —

Thank you for
inviting me to
speak at your
company's event.
I hope you enjoy
the book.

Unconventionally yours,

George.

Dec - 2013

The Unconventional Project Manager

The Unconventional Project Manager
Revenue Generation Strategies for Non-Salespeople
Copyright © 2012 by George L. Galaz
For information address SCA Press, 14511 Old Katy Rd,
Suite 364, Houston, Texas, 77079.
www.Sales4PMs.com
Printed in the United States of America.
FIRST EDITION
Library of Congress Cataloging-in-Publication Data
Galaz, George L.
The Unconventional Project Manager
Revenue Generation Strategies for Non-Salespeople
p. cm.
1. Project Management. 2. Sales. 3. Career Development. 4. Revenue Gen-
eration. I. Galaz, George. II. Title.

ISBN: 0615831818
ISBN-13: 9780615831817

The Unconventional Project Manager
Revenue Generation Strategies for Non-Salespeople

by
George Galaz Sr.

SCA Press

2012

I dedicate this work to my lovely wife and children, to my dear friends and life mentors; as well as to all the Unconventional Project Managers of the world.

Contents

Acknowledgements

I would like to thank all the people that with their support and encouragement contributed to making this book possible.

To all my dear friends and business associates thanks for all the long conversations, for believing in this project, for your ideas, for not letting me give up, for your words of wisdom, for the invaluable criticism, and for inspiring me to follow my dreams. I will not run the risk of missing anyone on a list, but you know who you are. To each one of you, THANK YOU!

Additionally, my dear wife and kids deserve all my gratitude for understanding my absences and for supporting me all the way.

A Message
To The Boardroom

If you are a corporate VP or CEO, this book will bring unmatched value to your organization. I know you are concerned with ensuring your company not only continues to meet revenue and profit targets as usual, but you also want your business to thrive, grow, and erode your competitors' position, so it can deliver even more value to your customers, shareholders, and employees.

I have yet to meet a C-level executive that does not want to improve fiscal performance. The one thing most top-floor executives have in common is the feeling that despite the efforts, the restructuring, the mergers and acquisitions, the new salespeople added to the team, and all the money spent on training, marketing, and advertising campaigns, results continue to decline or stay stagnant at best. The biggest concern expressed by Sales leaders during my research was that competitors were doing better every year.

If you lead a project-based company, I invite you to share this book with the project managers in your organization and see their reaction. I promise you many of them will have a very different appreciation for the work that you and your sales teams do every day to secure the orders that keep everybody busy and the machine moving.

More importantly, they will enthusiastically engage in various creative ways to help the business grow, not only by delivering outstanding project results, but also by actively participating in the business development strategy and for the first time having direct participation in the revenue-generating efforts of the corporation.

The Unconventional Project Manager™ is the first book of its kind, and it aims at completely disrupting the established paradigms and challenging the status quo in your organization to start bringing concrete results in a very short time. When used in conjunction with the in-house and web-based seminars, and with the coaching programs we custom design at Sales4PMs.com, the book will dramatically transform the way your company approaches revenue-generation today.

Unconventional Project Managers are a new breed of professionals that differentiate from traditional PMs by delivering tremendous amounts of value to their customers, building trust, and isolating their companies from the competition. The pages of this book will teach your PMs the necessary tools and strategies to help them become successful *Unconventional Project Managers* in record time and in doing so they will bring a massive contribution to the top-line of your corporation.

Thanks for the opportunity of contributing to write the next successful chapter of your company's history.

George Galaz, Sr.

Preface By Dave Jardine, Former President and Chairman Of Telvent North America

Computers and the Internet have created a global intelligent network enabling creativity, collaboration, and supply chain excellence. Business, social, and governance paradigms are ever changing, creating challenge and opportunity in market and supply systems.

Technology has not only reduced the client-vendor interaction time to nearly real-time, but has also opened the doors for customers to access a much broader range of possibilities when it comes to making purchasing decisions. Further, the impending demographic cliff with concomitant personal value-shifts affecting established processes across the enterprise are clearly affecting the way business is done, the way trust is established, and the timing of anticipated actions.

The marketplace is becoming increasingly more challenging, crowded with suppliers competing for an order and with customers demanding greater innovation every day. New products and services come and go, as competition drives prices down and commoditize within every industry. Now, more than ever companies need to differentiate to win in this new and tougher business world. However, different and better products are no longer enough; now customers are giving significant attention to distinctive engagements with the vendor community.

I have been working at customer value-creation my entire career, and have practiced and witnessed traditional product, solution, and value selling. I have seen my share of successes and failures, and the ups and downs of small and medium companies, as well as large multinational corporations. I have witnessed many companies grow, merge, become acquired, expand, downsize, and even disappear.

The top-line achievement has always been at the center of the business attention, and good project results have always been what differs winners from losers in the project-driven world.

Succeeding in today's marketplace is more challenging than ever for project-delivery businesses. Salespeople are having greater difficulty getting in front of customers today, which is forcing them to find creative ways to get the customer's attention and create preference for the products and services they sell.

George's proposal is an interesting and refreshing answer to this 21st Century business development predicament. Combining his experience as a successful project manager and sales leader, he is able to challenge traditional paradigms and offer winning strategies for improving corporate growth objectives.

I have always considered the project management role to be the lifeline for successful customer satisfaction and project success. I believe you would all agree that high customer satisfaction leads to growth and strong fiscal performance for long-term sustainability.

George presents us with *The Unconventional Project Manager*, a new breed of professional that not only understands project execution and customer success, but also embraces business development as a core competency to deliver outstanding *Value* to the corporation.

Selling is no longer a function exclusive to the sales team; companies' ability to generate repeat-business and loyal customers depends greatly on delivering successful projects, as measured by the customer's own definition of success. Crafting the next layer of value toward the customer's ultimate vision is the responsibility of more than just the sales team.

The amount of time the sales resources are able to spend face to face with potential clients is quickly diminishing and sales teams are struggling to find ways to open customer doors and present the value their company has to offer.

In this book, George disrupts the establishment and through memorable real-life examples he is able to show us how to address these challenges, creatively proposing new strategies for project managers, service engineers, technical teams, sales staff, and executives to work together and achieve greater success in the execution of a common business development plan.

In the simplest of terms, everyone has a role and a responsibility when it comes to growing customer satisfaction and top-line performance. I invite you to explore what *The Unconventional Project Manager* is all about and discover how the concepts and tactics within the twenty-seven chapters of this book can not only have a tremendous impact on your company's performance, but on your own professional career too.

Dave Jardine
Former President & Chairman
Telvent North America

Chapter 1

What Is The Unconventional Project Manager™ All About?

Many authors have written thousands of books in an attempt to give us the formula to increase revenue figures in the corporation. They typically write them for salespeople, some for beginners, and others for more seasoned professionals. In addition, many books are especially for non-salespeople; but never has a book been devoted in its entirety to the theory of the Project Manager as a *Revenue-Generating Agent*.

Why is this book for Project Managers and not for Salespeople? —First of all, let us clarify that this is not a sales book. This is a toolkit for project managers (and any other non-sales professional) to improve their business development skills, so they can take their careers to the next level and join the select group of successful *Unconventional* professionals that are helping their organizations thrive in the marketplace.

Secondly, more than a book, this work is a close look at the way we do things today in the corporate world, which is not very different from the way we did things years or even decades ago. Companies are in a never-ending quest to grow their top and bottom lines every year and they go about achieving that goal today in the very same way they have for decades.

This book is a challenge to the status quo and a proposal to creatively start approaching the issue from a different angle. I have interviewed dozens of corporate leaders and invariably all of them coincide in their appreciation that sales professionals are having increased difficulty in making a significant impact on the revenue volumes of the corporation; why? —Because salespeople will always lack two crucial factors when it comes to generating repeat business:

a.   They do not get enough time in front of customers; and

b.   Customers generally do not trust them!

These two aspects are the main reasons given by Sales VPs when trying to explain business decline. Sales staff is having a difficult time securing meetings with potential and existing customers. This explains why we observe an increased volume of recruiting activity in this area, where one of the most valued assets a candidate can have are his relationships to open doors and secure meetings. Business leaders slowly understand that this fact does not necessarily mean guaranteed success. Would you buy from another company simply because a salesperson you know now works there?

Most sales books and training material attack the issue by trying to teach or reinforce basic sales competencies, rather than by analyzing why the majority of salespeople are not consistent at bringing in new orders. The traditional approach consists of teaching account-planning processes, time management strategies, and showing us how to improve our cold-calling, follow up, presentation, negotiation, and closing skills. These are all very important competencies for any sales professional, but they are not enough to have any significant impact on the corporate balance sheet—at least not to the extent corporations expect today.

The transforming theories presented in the pages of this book will analyze typical project sales cycles and will study how and why our traditional sales approach continues to fail, time after time. *The Unconventional Project Manager*™ was conceived for those that—given the nature of their work—spend most of their time building and delivering what salespeople sold in the first place. Such is the case of the Project Manager.

This is <u>not</u> a book about running successful projects, nor is it about increasing figures by exploiting or abusing the dangerous change-order business practice. *The Unconventional Project Manager*™ is a powerful tool created purposely for non-sales professionals and primarily for project managers, service engineers, and for that matter any technical person who spends time in front of customers delivering value by solving their problems. Nonetheless, the real power of the tools presented in the following pages comes from the amalgamated efforts of all stakeholders in the organization.

Business development is a strategy, perhaps the most important of all corporate strategies there is. As such, companies should plan and execute this strategy jointly with all members of technical, project management, sales, executive, customer service, marketing, and product development teams.

In fact, we strongly recommend that all stakeholders in your organization read this book at some point, and later meet to discuss it. All revenue-generating strategies presented in this book always work best if all key players in your organization collaborate in planning, implementing, and executing them.

The author spent the first half of his professional career managing large technology-intense projects around the world. During the second half, he became an accomplished sales leader and a sought-after business development and marketing consultant.

This unique mix of experiences gave him a broad exposure to what became a very evident problem: Salespeople were not delivering consistent results, while few project managers, service engineers, and technicians were doing something unique, which allowed them to be increasingly successful at bringing in new orders. In fact, the author's own transition from managing projects to a successful career in sales happened because of this very same aspect.

Technology, engineering, financial, insurance, and construction companies are the ideal playfield for observing this phenomenon. In fact, any business with a sales force and a project execution group is a good candidate for putting the principles taught in *The Unconventional Project Manager* into practice.

This book proposes a complete transformation of the way we approach business development today in project-based organizations. My paradigm is that PMs and salespeople should be trained to develop to their full potential and both should be integral part of a carefully designed strategy to bring-in more business.

The following pages will illustrate how managing the *Time & Event* variables of your business is perhaps the most important strategy you can implement to consistently increase revenues in your organization. A dear friend, sales leader, and entrepreneur, once told me in Bogotá, Colombia:

"Every event in business has a moment in time. The key is to learn to manage the timing at which those events take place. Once you learn to put the right resources in front of the customer at the right time, you will find that magic formula you have been searching for in order to increase your sales numbers."

Understanding the role of project managers and salespeople is important, but gaining a true comprehension of the timing for placing each resource before our customers is critical to business growth. We will analyze this simple but powerful strategy later in the book.

Through the utilization of real life examples that the reader can easily relate to, we will illustrate each of the concepts covered in the book. You will get an understanding of how the customer's mind works and you will learn what turns clients on and off during the vendor selection process. You will also discover what PMs have that salespeople will <u>never</u> have. We will briefly discuss basic aspects of marketing, advertising, and the impact of branding in the revenue-generation cycle, as well as the role the PM can play to improve results.

Additionally, we will dedicate a complete chapter to study Value, how customers understand it, and simple—yet powerful—strategies you can implement to improve *Value Dialog*, something even experienced sales professionals struggle with. We will cover various customer service scenarios, analyzing the difference project managers and delivery teams can make in creating memorable customer experiences.

Later in the book, a few chapters are dedicated to reviewing the important role of the PM as a social entity, as well as different cases of customer retention, loyalty, and advocacy. Throughout the book, we will emphasize how each topic can enrich the reader's career by providing the necessary tools to implement the concepts learned and quickly differentiate from colleagues and peers.

We will also discuss the three business development models and will analyze how project managers can leverage their roles to make a massive contribution to the organization. In terms of strategy we will analyze a popular board game and will visit with Sun Tzu, a Chinese army general that more than 2,000 years ago wrote what is perhaps the most relevant book in business strategy today.

We will review project sales cycles, project pricing models, incentives, reward systems, and how to deal with difficult customers. Additionally we will discuss the importance of smart account management practices, and many other interesting aspects of modern project business development, including the pyramidal organization strategy, and various effective ways to differentiate yourself, your company, and its products from the competition.

We will see what successful projects really look like, will take a careful look at our own assumptions and their consequences, and will learn what Isaac Newton and the modern corporation have in common.

Once again, the intent of this book is not to turn project managers into salespeople, but rather to provide PMs with the necessary tools to help them understand the criticality of their role in the **Need Creation** process, which ultimately is the basis for sustainable *revenue generation*.

The book is purposely concise, as it was designed for a quick read. Its language is simple and to the point, and it is organized in brief chapters, so they can easily be used as a reference tool any time.

Whether you received this book as a gift, bought it online or at the bookstore, or obtained it during one of the author's public appearances, we truly hope you enjoy learning why non-salespeople hold the keys to unlocking the most successful years of your organization.

Chapter 2
The Customer Mind

Every purchase decision begins with either a need or desire. At the individual level, we also initiate the purchasing process of a product or service simply because we have a need or desire. Often the financial aspects of the purchase take a secondary role and we leave them for later analysis. More often than necessary, we decide to acquire things we cannot afford, or feel pushed into buying things we do not need.

During this process, we observe behavioral changes that help us convince ourselves that we need what we desire; and we are even capable of elaborating a creative list of arguments to help us justify the purchase decision of such products or services. Marketing and advertising play a critical role in this process, for the various manufacturers and suppliers of literally millions of products and services are fighting endlessly to get our attention, to entice us to desire their products and ultimately transform that desire into a feeling of need. In other words, they are executing a carefully crafted Need Creation strategy.

Let us assume for a moment that you *want* to build a swimming pool in your house backyard. You *dream* about it for weeks, you discuss it with your spouse; you spend hours outside imagining how the finished product would look like and how your children and friends will enjoy the new addition to the property. You know the project would be costly; however, you start creating a mental list of good reasons to go forward with it:

- It would increase the resell value of the house.
- The kids would spend more time at home.

- You could take less vacation trips and stay home in the summers instead.
- Relatives would visit more often.
- You could save on energy by using less AC while you are outside.
- Family would spend more time together.
- It will be a grandchildren's magnet.
- Palm trees would look nice behind the pool.
- Etc.

You know nothing about the process of building a pool, nor do you have a clear idea as to how much it would cost. What do you do next? —You dedicate yourself to the task of finding a pool construction company. You search the Internet, community magazines, and you ask friends and neighbors for tips. Finally, you have a list of five candidates (bidders). You call them up one by one and schedule appointments for them to send their sales representatives to your house and evaluate your project.

During the meetings, you and your spouse explain your *desire* for a swimming pool, show the salespeople the location in the backyard, and ask them for ideas and recommendations. In the end, three vendors came to offer their services. Each brought their own advantages and disadvantages to the table, and soon you faced the difficult task of making a *Purchasing Decision*.

Following is a description of what could have actually happened during your meetings:

Company-A:
- The salesperson brought some photocopies to introduce the company.
- He showed you some paper pictures of previous jobs.
- He took some measurements in the backyard.
- He performed an *elevator pitch* to convince you that his company is the best in the market.
- Drew a sketch by hand of what the pool would look like.

- Pulled a calculator and jotted down the price for the project and completion time.
- He offered to put you in contact with some of his happy customers.

Total meeting time: 1 hour.

Company-B:
- The representative brought glossy, full-color brochures to introduce the company.
- She showed you some pictures and videos of previous jobs on her laptop computer.
- She took some measurements in the backyard.
- She showed you a slide presentation to convince you they are the experts in the business.
- Drew a sketch of what the pool would look like using specialized 3D computer software.
- The same software created a costing page from which she gave you a quote for the job.
- She left some recommendation letters from previous customers.

Total meeting time: 1.5 hours.

Company-C:
- The person brought a briefcase that he set on the floor by his side.
- He asked you and your spouse a number of questions, while he made some notes.
- He learned you had no previous experience with building a pool.
- He proceeded to educate you about the pool building process.
- He also covered all aspects of operating and maintaining a pool.
- He shared various videos on his tablet device that showed the construction steps.

- You learned about every aspect, every material, every stage, and every risk involved.
- He discussed with you different alternatives and the pros and cons of each one.
- After the discussion you all agree on three possible options for the pool:
  - o Thrifty
  - o Nice Compromise
  - o Dream Oasis
- He took detail measurements in the backyard and suggested ideal location.
- He promised to send a complete proposal the next morning.
- Indicated his price would be firm, no surprise charges later on and clearly indicated any exclusions.

Total meeting time: 2.5 hours.

Note:
I shall reference and analyze this simple example in detail throughout the forthcoming chapters and it will help me illustrate many of the various concepts I will introduce later in the book.

Chapter 3

What Do PMs Have That Salespeople Will Never Have?

The three pool construction companies visited the home with the same objective. Did you notice how the last representative never opened his briefcase and never even mentioned his products or company names? He actually never pulled any marketing material whatsoever.

Company-A's salesperson utilized a *cookie-cutter* sales approach. He treated you like any other client and your dream or *desire* as any other job. This salesperson failed at differentiating himself from the competition and at offering *value*.

Company-B's employee managed to impress you with the use of some technology in the design and costing of your pool. However, she also failed at differentiating herself and at bringing real *Value* to the exercise. More importantly, both vendors failed at one of the most important aspects of selling, building *Trust*. We will come back to this aspect in a later chapter, where we will analyze the elements of *Distinctive Value*.

Both salespeople have one thing in common: They both tried to *pitch* or promote their company and their pool construction services, which is a very typical and natural selling behavior. They both spent energy trying to convince you and your spouse that their companies were the best at building pools.

To the contrary, Company-C's representative did not waste time trying to sell you anything. He recognized that you—like most homeowners—have little to no previous experience in building pools. He capitalized on that fact and proceeded to execute what experts do best: <u>Educate</u> you on the ins and outs of building a swimming pool.

In doing so he gained access to one of the most precious and scarce elements there is: **YOUR TIME**. Once the meeting was over—and as you walked the representative to the door—he gave you his business card. Only after he left you realized his card read *"John Smith, Project Manager."* What you did not know is that the salesperson that was supposed to visit you had an emergency and could not make the meeting on time and asked one of the company's PMs in the area to come by and visit you in his place.

After dinner, you discussed the experience with your spouse and quickly agreed that Company-C was by far the one you wanted to hire, simply because you felt you could trust the person they sent, and because he demonstrated to be the most knowledgeable in the process of building pools. *"He seemed honest and not pushy at all"* was your spouse's comment. In fact, he never tried to sell you anything! You have the feeling his company may not offer the lowest price, but you are confident your budget will fit at least one of the three options he will present you with tomorrow.

As promised, first thing in the morning you receive an email from Company-C's project manager with their proposal:

- It contained all three options with full color renderings and fly-through videos.
- Each option listed benefits and disadvantages, like consumables and energy costs.
- Each option included detail, per item pricing.
- Each option considered a clear execution schedule.

There is no question about the fact that Company-C was your preferred option, and although it did not offer the lowest price, you decided to build the *Nice Compromise* pool with them. Company-C was the vendor that gave you the most peace of mind and at a cost close to your budget. You also valued their written commitment to no surprise price increases.

The key take away points about Company-C's approach are:

1. The representative never tried to sell you anything. Instead of *pushing,* he *pulled* by asking smart questions (see chapter on *Push vs. Pull Theory*).

2. He spent time *educating* you about the pool building process (*Trust*).

3. He maximized the amount of time he had before you.

4. He kept his company's marketing material in the briefcase (did not *push*).

Once construction started, Company-C assigned the same person as the actual project manager for the job, and he ensured you were involved throughout the whole process. He continued to educate you about each step and in the end walked you through the complete pool operation and maintenance procedures. Upon completion, not only did you have a beautiful pool, but also you were very knowledgeable about the pool's construction, operation, and maintenance processes.

Later your neighbor asked if you could recommend a good pool contractor, and so did your friends and relatives. It seems like Company-C is getting a lot of repeat business through you. Leveraging technical resources and putting them in front of the customer at the right time is the best strategy to not only secure immediate orders, but also future business.

Chapter 4

Creating Need

The practice of motivating and moving people to buy something (whether they think they need it or not) is known as *Creating Need*. The salespeople that knock on your door Saturday morning and try to convince you of buying a vacuum cleaner are utilizing this very same strategy. Through impressive demonstrations, they recite a carefully studied script designed to show you that this machine is precisely what you *need* to solve your cleaning problems and reduce energy costs, while at the same time help save the planet, for example.

If the feelings of desire, wish, or dream are already present, then the *Need Creation* exercise is very easy or not required at all. Instead, the strategy of *Need Justification* comes into play and the salesperson will leverage the feelings in your head to drive you to a purchasing decision.

For example, you have a flat screen TV set in perfectly working condition, but you want the latest model that offers new cool features you *wish* to have. You come up with a list of good reasons to *justify* the expense of buying a new TV set, even though you already have a unit in good working order. My wife is an expert at convincing me why she needs a new pair of shoes, or a new designer bag, for example. That is what I call persuasive *Need Justification*.

The traditional sales process lends itself to exploiting the sense of urgency and inclusion. For example, if the same salesperson introduced above tells you *"we are offering a 20% discount on all vacuum cleaner models, but only valid if you purchase today..."* That is a *push* strategy designed to give you a sense of urgency, so you cannot resist the temptation of getting such a good deal.

Similarly, the salesperson could say something like *"five of your neighbors in this area have already taken advantage of today's special pricing..."* Experts have designed this statement to make you feel excluded should you think that buying the product is not a good idea. You do not want to be the exception among your neighbors, and you too want to be the proud owner of such a good product at such a good price.

Salespeople shift to Need Creation strategies whenever the potential buyer has no intention (or desire) to purchase the type of product or service they are selling. Without the *need* factor there will never be a purchasing decision element in the equation, and the salesperson will never get the order.

There are Need Creation examples all around our daily lives. The municipal water our parents and grandparents drank just a few decades ago never presented an issue. Through marketing and advertising campaigns, filtered water companies were able to educate us about the presence of various metals and minerals in municipal water, which in turn created a sense for urgency and need in our heads, so much so that we turned spring water into a basic necessity rather than a luxury item.

The project world

In professional selling, Need Creation is particularly important. Often our customers know very well what they want (desire) and need. However, sometimes they are routinely dealing with many issues and frustrations and they get used to the way things work today, failing to investigate whether there are easier, better, or more efficient ways for managing those problems.

The professional salesperson is an expert at identifying customers' stress (what keeps them awake at night) and presenting them with products, services, and solutions that promise to take that stress away and solve their problems for good. In this case, the customer has a passive or dormant need, as he or she is so accustomed to doing things the same way, that he or she does not realize the need for a better way. When a product or service that radically improves the results is introduced, need is quickly created and the sales process begins. We can observe situations like these typically during consultative selling.

However, there is only one problem with this picture; customers usually do not trust salespeople. Why? –Well, because they are salespeople! If the truth is to be said, we hate opening the door to a vacuum cleaner sales representative, right? –Well, our customers do too.

Not everyone is in the best position to create need (remember *Time & Event?*). In fact, in most cases—and especially in the professional selling environment—the salesperson is in the worst position to create need effectively.

The art of creating need is all about influencing the minds and souls of our potential buyers. In order to achieve this, the prospective buyer needs to *let you in* first. This is where the *Trust* component comes into play. If they do not trust you, you will never get past the front door.

The role of the project manager

Customers perceive project managers and the technical experts that work in project and service teams as the only ones capable of solving their problems. When something breaks, they come and fix it. When they need expert technical advice, they provide the answers. When confronted with multiple options, they shed light on the best alternative. Technical experts and PMs are the customer's allies, their consultants, and their peers. Buyers, on the other hand, usually perceive salespeople as the enemy, the evil entity that wants to trick them into buying something they do not necessarily need.

Both, the PM and the salesperson could very well recommend to solve a given problem with the same product or service, but the prospective buyer will typically trust better the advice of the PM or technical expert, instead of that of the sales representative.

In our swimming pool construction project example, the project manager attended a meeting with a potential buyer merely by accident. Yet the results are evident. In this case, an already justified wish or desire created the need. All the PM had to do was build Trust (keeping his briefcase closed and educating the client) and reinforce the idea that building a pool was a sound investment. More importantly, he was successful at removing any uncertainty factors from the client's mind and convincing the couple that his bid was going to be the one with the lowest risk possible, giving written assurances that price will never increase during project execution.

He got the order that very night even before he submitted the proposal. Company-C's project manager was the best salesperson that day, and through that customer, he acquired five more deals in the same year (Advocacy). His boss' natural reaction would be to promote him and make him a salesperson, right? –Well, not quite. Ideally, this project manager would remain a PM and his employer would reward him accordingly.

The biggest mistake would be to remove him from his position of trust and give him a salesperson hat (and a business card for that matter). The key to his success with this deal was the fact that he was not pushing for the order; he was simply helping his prospective buyer understand the pool building process, and almost naively managed to build incredible amounts of trust, which in turn helped him secure the order for his company. He treated the customer the way he would have liked others to treat him in a similar situation.

This last aspect is very important in professional business development. In most cases, the people that are best at building trust and executing a *Consultative Sales Strategy* are those who do not even realize are doing it. In fact, I would not be surprised at all if the salesperson that was supposed to attend that meeting with the client that day, purposely sent the PM in his place, knowing that it would be the best Time & Event management strategy, given the circumstances.

A corporate case example

What would the situation look like if the client has no dreams or desires? How can you create need then? Let us illustrate with an enterprise-oriented situation: You are the salesperson for a plant-optimization software company. You have identified ABC Brewery Inc. as a potential buyer who might be in need of your solution. You organized a technical seminar at a conveniently located hotel downtown and invited the client to the *Optimization Day* event.

Through your homework you have learned that ABC Brewery Inc. balances the operational aspects of their plant by utilizing a rudimentary spreadsheet-based system, which was created in-house many years ago, and it is as time consuming as it is inaccurate. You brought Natasha with you—the subject matter technical expert—and you decided to introduce her to the customer to initiate the educating process, which you hope will help her build *trust* and ultimately drive the customer to the purchasing decision scenario you need.

The expert spent two hours talking about the advantages of having a cloud-based solution that automatically optimizes the logistics and operational aspects of the plant. From the supply chain equation to the maintenance and downtime scenarios, including just-in-time inventories, power optimization, and a predictive model that can quickly adjust throughput based on variables such as weather, holidays, and other market conditions.

During her presentation, you observed your clients' eyes opening and their jaws literally dropping in disbelief. They will finally be able to sleep well at night again. At last, someone was able to identify their stress and present them with a viable option to make it go away. There was actually a better way of doing things out there. For the first time a professional was speaking about their problem without trying to persuade them to buy anything!

Key aspects to this scenario:

    a)   Prospective buyer was not actively looking for a solution.
    b)   Prospective buyer was content with the current method.
    c)   Prospective buyer did not (consciously) have a need or desire.
    d)   Salesperson took the *back seat*.
    e)   Technical expert was in front of client to deliver *Value* and build *Trust*.
    f)   Technical expert never mentioned or demonstrated an actual product.
    g)   A new *desire* was born and it immediately turned into a *need*.
    h)   Prospective buyer asked if you had such a product and to arrange for a demonstration.

Regardless of whether need is created out of a pre-existing wish or desire, or simply by making evident the existence of an issue or problem that hinders efficiency, optimization, or returns; this strategy is perhaps the most important tool that anyone can use to generate new business.

Also, the realization that not always the salesperson is the best resource to be put in front of the potential buyer and the importance of building trust, are two of the best well kept secrets to repeat business. The careful management of Time & Event is a tactic that when well played, yields astonishing results.

Once again, often project managers and subject matter experts—not salespeople—are best equipped for building trust with prospective buyers and for creating need for your company's products and services. We will discuss more on this topic in subsequent chapters.

Chapter 5

What Business Is Your Customer In?

This chapter is going to be very brief, but it is important to ensure this point is very clear, and it is important that you never forget this basic fact. In the examples above, what business were Companies A, B, and C in? –Building swimming pools, right?

Now, in the case of client ABC Brewery Inc., what was the main business of the company that employed you? –Delivering plant optimization software, correct?

- Wrong!

Unless your customer is a church, a government, or any non-profit organization, they are all in only one line of business, the business of <u>making money</u>.

This also applies to your own organization. Your company is not in the business of building power plants, bridges, refineries, airports, shopping malls, pipelines, crude production facilities, houses, or advanced software applications. Your company is not in the business of selling customized credit or financing solutions, nor is it in the business of designing and selling complex insurance models. Your company is in the business of making money (I hope this does not come as a big surprise to you).

It is very important to remember this fundamental aspect of business every time we are getting ready to engage a prospective buyer or an existing customer for that matter. Both, your company and your customer's organizations exist with the sole purpose of being profitable. Even some government or state-run organizations have a mandate for profits, like National Oil & Gas companies, for example.

Even in the case of non-profit organizations, the same is true to some extent. Although they are not seeking financial growth, they have a financial concern. In fact, all non-profit organizations have a budget, and when purchasing goods, executing projects, or allocating charitable grants they must be very careful not to come short or exceed those budgets. In other words, for them a break-even outcome is the equivalent to a profitable result in the for-profit world.

Your job is to ensure you do whatever you can to help that customer stay in budget and to deliver a break-even point solution. That is how non-profit organizations measure success.

Nevertheless, for the purpose of this book, we will assume your company, as well as your customers and prospective buyers are clearly in the business of making money. What companies build and sell in the marketplace (products or services) are the means to making money. Never confuse the end with the means.

An airline company, for example, uses airplanes, airport facilities, computer systems, jet fuel, air and ground employees, logistics experts, and passengers to make money. The revenues an airline generates (passenger tickets and cargo contracts) are used to offset its operational costs. If the latter are greater than the former, we have an airline in trouble. If the opposite occurs then we have a profitable airline. This simple equation applies to all for-profit companies in the world, regardless of the industry they serve, or the products or services they sell.

Many elements come into play when determining the profitability of an airline, like the breakeven point per flight, which is the number of seats that the company must sell per particular aircraft and route to make that specific flight profitable. Some routes are more profitable than others are, and some particular flights within those routes are more profitable too, depending on season, date, and time of travel, weather, etc.

Customer service plays a pivotal role in the profitability and sustainability of an airline company, for unhappy passengers can spread the word easily and rapidly on the Internet about their bad experiences with the company, asking readers to stay away and prefer other providers. In a competitive marketplace where margins are so tight, businesses cannot afford to lose one single customer, which can have exponential results if they are unhappy or dissatisfied.

In later chapters we are going to analyze what project-based companies and project managers can do to help ensure a positive customer experience and to turn frustrated clients into satisfied customers not only willing to come back for more, but also to advocate for our products, services, and people.

Chapter 6

The Branded Project Manager

Though one can write a full book on the subject of marketing and advertising, I want to cover some very basic aspects of these two complementing disciplines at least. Despite the fact that most likely you have no *"wish"* or *"desire"* to read about these topics, I believe it is important that we have a leveled foundation in this regard to cover other concepts later in the book.

More importantly, we will highlight the important role you and your team can (should) play to help your organization maximize returns on these investments.

The marketing and advertising functions can easily be confused and often blurred into one single discipline. What is important to realize is that—when executed properly—both marketing and advertising play a pivotal role in the successful implementation of business development strategies; and project managers, service, and technical team members are in the best position to support the successful execution of those.

The job of business developers becomes significantly easier if corporations take the marketing and advertising functions seriously, and if they execute the respective campaigns in close coordination with the sales and project groups.

If you are a project manager or a subject matter expert that spends time in front of customers, then it is crucial that you understand how you fit between these two disciplines, so you can better contribute to securing future business for your company, and therefore creating the results that will catapult you into new heights in your professional career.

The best way to understand the role of each function is to address the concept of *branding* first. A brand can be your company name, your product name, or both. Let us take a popular brand as an example: Apple Inc. is the multinational corporation behind the Apple® brand. We all recognize that brand today thanks to the tremendous, ingenious, and sometimes risky marketing and advertising efforts of Steve Jobs and collaborators.

All those efforts put together are what we call the art and science of *branding*. Therefore, in essence, your company or product names alone are not a brand. Only when a company carries out a concerted effort to give *meaning* to those names (brand positioning) we can talk about a true brand. When a company executes its branding strategy successfully, the result should be a clearly recognizable brand by its targeted audience.

When a name is easily and clearly associated with a product, service, or activity by those in the target audience (or niche), then we have a true brand. A brand can also be a proper name, like Michael Schumacher or Tiger Woods, for example. In these cases, they are easily associated with the sports they practice professionally, and therefore they are their own brand.

Apple does not simply mean computers, music players, smart phones, or tablet devices. Apple also signifies quality products and beautiful, simple, and functional designs, at least for many people (millions of people). There is no hard definition for a brand, for each individual will interpret the meaning of the brand differently, depending on various personal, social, anthropological, and even psychological factors. The magic of an effective branding strategy is that the brand should have a somewhat similar meaning for everybody in the target group.

In fact Apple was so successful in the execution of their branding strategies that a few of their products defined the category there are in. iPod® and iPad® are clear examples of this achievement. Most airline flight attendants invite passengers to turn their iPods and iPads off prior to take off and landing, not their *"music players"* and *"tablet devices."* In the early '80s, the brand Walkman® from Sony® meant portable music player. Similarly, their brand Betamax® meant household videocassette player for a number of years, until JVC® later introduced the VHS® format and competition drove prices down.

Palm Pilot® reached a similar level of brand recognition in the '90s, but soon contemporary competitors surpassed it. For a few years, Palm Pilot meant PDA (Personal Digital Assistant) in the entire world. Later, the product's inventor rebranded the gadget simply as Palm® handhelds due to a trademark dispute with another company, before selling the company to HP®. All these examples prove two of the most fundamental principles in marketing:

a) Being first to market does not guarantee perennial success; and
b) For a good product with good branding to stay successful, it must remain in the cutting edge of product evolution and innovation, always.

Critics may have attacked Apple for releasing too many new versions of the same product too often. In my opinion, this very risky maneuver has kept the company at the pinnacle of their niche for many years. Experts argue that without the massive anticipation that comes with each release, the brand would have suffered, and competing products would have been able to erode Apple's market dominance.

Apple's original logo used in 1976

The only problem with innovation is that competing companies quickly come up with a "me too" version of the same or very similar product. It is not rare to see "me too" products surpass those released by the companies that invested heavily in inventing and developing them. This explains why Apple develops every new product with such secrecy, so they can be first to market every time, fueling the brand (and stock price) to record levels.

Why can a company be so successful when bringing a revolutionary product to market and so quickly have an imitator doing the same? The answer to this question lies in marketing. Apple is one of very few companies that are brilliant not only at innovating and introducing new products to the marketplace—often defining a new category altogether—, but also at protecting the brand and remaining at the pinnacle of its niche.

All the growth that comes with the successful introduction of a new product can quickly crumble to the ground if organizations do not properly design and execute their marketing strategies.

Apple's latest logo, used since 1998

How does this look in your own company?

So far, we have discussed popular and massive brands, referred to as *Consumer Product* brands. Let us now analyze more targeted or niche-oriented brands. Think of your own company and the products they sell. Are they massive or niche-oriented products? Let us assume you work for a company that manufactures and sells specialized smoke detectors for airplanes. Let us call your company *ACME* and the product *ACME Smart* Smoke Detector.

In the case of target niche branding, the marketing and advertising strategies must be very different from those executed by Apple or Coca-Cola®, of course. The objective here is completely different. Instead of positioning the brand massively, the goal is to gain recognition in a very specific group of people. In the case of ACME, the target group is aeronautical companies and aircraft manufactures, and of course the professionals that work for those organizations.

To reach their audiences with a brand message, consumer product companies use massive advertising campaigns. Newspapers and magazine ads, radio announcements, TV commercials, the Internet, etc., are all forms of advertising media. Apple and Coca-Cola are famous for their creative TV commercials; but what about our friends at ACME? Have you seen their latest commercial on TV? Household consumers are not their target niche, and therefore spending advertising dollars there would not be effective.

Instead, they use specialized media to reach out to their target audience. In this specific example, they may place ads on aeronautical and aircraft maintenance magazines, for example.

Let us talk about *marketing*. Is it necessary?

Advertising alone cannot achieve branding objectives. Marketing is essential to completing the branding picture. For a vertical brand like ACME, the utilization of a comprehensive marketing strategy is fundamental to the overall success of the brand and the company for that matter. For this type of niche-oriented companies, marketing is often more important than advertising.

The presence of the brand in the main aeronautical and aircraft trade-show circuit, for example, is unquestionable for a company like this. A trade show or technology fair is the perfect opportunity to promote the brand and bring it closer to the target audience that visits these events.

Publishing and presenting technical papers at symposiums and similar events is also an excellent opportunity for positioning a vertical technology brand before a target niche audience. The design of a clear and effective logo, as well as the creation of brochures, business cards, websites, and mailing materials is also another component of marketing.

Again, in our aeronautical and aircraft example, the company may choose to organize a technology seminar and invite customers and potential buyers to learn about a new product. This is another form of marketing. Nowadays the utilization of web-based seminars (or *"webinars"*) is also very common.

At **Sales4PMs**™, for example, we provide Sales, Project Management, and Service teams with tailored in-house and web-based seminars and coaching programs, designed to help corporations of all sizes reach their revenue growth and market share objectives.

When does the salesperson come in?

Selling is the effort of convincing a customer to purchase a product or service. If you are a salesperson, your job is to get customers in your territory to buy your company's products and services, and you must leverage your company's marketing, branding, and advertising resources to accomplish that goal.

If you are in marketing, your job is to understand the target audience for your company's product or service. Know what product they want or need, how they want it, and how much they are willing to pay for it. It is also your job to prepare all supporting material for the sales group (brochures, slideshows, giveaways, uniforms, trade show booths, press releases, etc.)

Who is responsible for branding if companies typically outsource the advertising function to expert agencies? –Some may say that branding is a marketing function, and in many ways this is 100% correct. However, in my personal opinion, branding is the amalgamation of all the company's activities and efforts, including marketing, advertising, sales, product development and innovation, delivery, customer service, warranty, etc.

In other words, branding is a philosophy, a way of conducting business. True branding takes place only when everybody in the organization is performing their role with the company's brand(s) in mind.

If customer service at Apple was a terrible experience, for example, I am sure the brand strength would be very different today, regardless of everything else.

Chapter 7

Understanding Value

So far, we have covered how to create need, how to build trust, and how to justify the transformation of a wish or desire into a need. Now we will study how to *Create Value*.

We should not confuse Value creation with creating need. Whenever we purchase something, we are buying value. When we choose a brand of beer over another, we are buying value. When we prefer a particular computer brand, we are paying for value. In our pool construction project example, Company-C was delivering value. In fact, all three contractors were offering some value, but only one was able to deliver value the way the customer understood it.

Why is this important? Value is a subjective matter; each individual *perceives* Value differently. The way I value drinking a bottle of beer may be very different from the way you do. Furthermore, the value I assign to drinking one particular kind (or brand) of beer might also be different from the value you place on drinking that same kind or brand of beer (you may dislike my kind of beer and prefer a different type).

We all exercise value calculation when making purchasing decisions. We can buy a brand new flat screen TV for $300 or $10,000. Both devices perform the same function: Displaying digital images on the screen for our entertainment.

One can observe a similar situation when selecting a car. We can buy a brand new car for $10,000, $15,000, $25,000, $50,000, $75,000, $150,000, and so on. They all perform the same function of transporting us from point A to point B, correct? So, where is the difference? Why do we choose one car over another or one TV set over another? —Because we assign different levels of *Value* to different characteristics of the product or service we are buying.

In other words, what is important to you may not necessarily be important to me, and vice versa. We can also explore the fact that we place different value levels on the same product or service depending on the circumstances we are in. Here is an example:

Peter decided to purchase two vehicles for the family, a lower-end car to take him to and from work on a daily basis, go grocery shopping, etc., and a higher-end vehicle for special occasions only, like going to formal events, parties, etc. Both cars serve the same purpose of transporting him and his family, but one is more *valuable* in one situation than the other is.

He perceives driving the expensive luxury car to work every day as a bad decision, since he knows the vehicle will depreciate faster with the amount of mileage he will drive each year. In this case, he values more the ability to drive a less expensive car to work every day, so he can protect the investment he made on the luxury vehicle.

Similarly, he may assign a significant amount of value to the opportunity of arriving at his favorite restaurant, bar, or club in style, so he cherishes the chance of owning a more luxurious vehicle, which—if only driven occasionally—will depreciate very slowly as opposed to driving it all the time.

In the example of the flat screen television, we may be talking about our appreciation for different features or quality. The more sophisticated features a unit has, the more expensive it will be. Similarly, at higher quality and durability, higher is the price. Depending on how much we *value* those aspects (features, quality, and durability) is how much we will be willing to spend on a new TV set.

In the case of the two cars, Peter not only is buying quality, reliability, and dependability; he is also buying *"status."* The inexpensive car will also take him to the fancy restaurant and back in the same amount of time. In fact, even a low-end vehicle nowadays has high quality standards, so he is not concerned with the vehicle breaking down half way to his destination.

So, why someone would spend more money on a car that serves the same purpose as the less expensive one? The answer is simple: Because that person gives a significant amount of *value* to feeling special and to the ability of arriving at the restaurant (or bar, or nightclub) in style, or at least in the way he or she understands style (another subjective concept).

This also explains why some people are willing to pay five, ten, even one hundred times more for a particular brand of watch over another (remember *branding?*). It is a simple device, which only purpose is to tell us the time. Nonetheless, a more expensive watch not only tells us the time, it is also a piece of jewelry, a status symbol, one that makes some people feel special. In this case, we value more the feeling of special and the status symbol, than the basic function of knowing what time it is.

How can consumers perceive one product or service as being able to deliver status, or the notion of feeling special? It all boils down to branding. The conjugation of marketing, advertising, product development and innovation, plus the branding strategy, is what gives meaning to a specific brand.

A watch company may position their brand higher than other brands because they understand that some people value the notion of feeling special more than others do. Think about it, we see it everywhere, all the time: Expensive pens, mobile phones, watches, clothing, shoes, haircuts, hotels, restaurants, etc. Branding is the powerful tool that defines how the marketplace will perceive a product or service and how much consumers will be willing to pay for it.

Value in the service industry

Let us introduce a service concept into our examples, so you see how this applies beyond the typical product company. Let us assume you need to go to the airport to take a four-hour flight to another city. It is a 45-minute drive from your house to the airport and you have the following alternatives:

a) Drive your own car and pay for parking, gas, and depreciation.
b) Take a taxi.
c) Hire a luxury sedan at a premium.

Which option would you take? —Well, it depends, right? It depends on the value you place on the different aspects of transportation to the airport. Do you value more riding in the comfort and expected cleanness of a luxury vehicle over a regular cab? If you are on a business trip, flying in first class, and wearing a nice suit for an important meeting, perhaps yes (especially if your company is covering the fare). However, if you are on vacation, flying economy, and wearing your regular weekend jeans, perhaps it is harder to justify the expense of a luxury vehicle.

Some people may argue that regardless of the situation, nothing justifies the expense of hiring a luxury car for something as trivial as a point-to-point ride. Now, what if tomorrow is your wedding anniversary and you are taking your spouse to a fine restaurant? You are both going to look amazing, sparkling in elegant clothes. Would you want to make the occasion even more memorable by impressing your spouse with a luxury sedan, or even a limo waiting at the door?

The point is that *Value* is a relative term and it is in nature very subjective. We all perceive value differently and we may change how we value things over time, depending on the circumstances and our own evolution as individuals.

Thirsty for value

Imagine you are lost in the middle of the desert, it is 2:00 PM, and you have had no water for the last two days. You have no idea where you are, it is scorching hot, and it could be days before you find your way out. How much would you be willing to pay for a bottle of water? Would you be willing to pay a premium for such a commodity product, which is readily available in the city? Would you pay $10, maybe $50? Would you pay $100, perhaps $300? I bet not only would you pay anything for that bottle of water, but also you would do so more than enthusiastically.

All of a sudden, the value you put on that bottle of water sharply increased, simply because the circumstances have changed. Nothing is more precious than what is scarce and marketers know this very well. Just a few days earlier, it would have been not a big problem emptying a bottle of water down the drain and now you are on your knees willing to pay a fortune for a few ounces of the same commodity.

Modern marketing has taken the concept of scarcity to a completely new place, in order to drive prices (our willingness to pay) to levels never seen before. Today our social definition of scarcity has evolved from the orthodox *"total or partial disappearance (slow or sudden) of a product or service from the marketplace"* to the 21st Century phenomenon of *"the anxious expectation of the arrival of the new cool product or service everybody is talking about."* Thousands of people of all ages are willing to camp outside storefronts to be the first ones in securing a newly released gadget, despite the fact that it will continue to be available for the same price the day and the week after, even months, if not years later.

In my opinion, Steve Jobs took this new scarcity marketing technique to new heights with the launch of the original iPod. It was the first product of its kind in the market, yet everybody knew about it, and everybody was *thirsty* for it. From that day on, every version of it—including the unification of the mobile telephone with a music player and organizer (aka iPhone®)—was a global event of epic proportions. These high levels of expectation and the buzz that took place prior to launch day, is what has allowed Apple to demand a higher price for the devices we buy today.

In the last few years we have witnessed the most perfect combination of value selling and scarcity strategies ever exercised by a single company in a relatively short time. Apple made its products scarce even before launch day and we all contributed to the campaign by putting tremendous amounts of value in owning them. People were (are) willing to pay a premium for the special feeling of owning one of those little gadgets.

Jobs' audacity and boldness is studied today at most advertising and business schools all over the world, and people will continue to study it for decades to come.

Chapter 8

EV + DV * T = PS

I have read many books on the subject of *Value Creation*, but in my opinion only one author has been able to explain it in the most simple and effective terms. In his book, *Becoming Preferred* ™ my dear friend Michael Vickers (www.MichaelVickers.com) delivers excellent examples of effective value creation. I highly recommend reading his book, which in my opinion is a must read for anybody that is serious about becoming a sales leader or an expert at delivering unique *Value,* and therefore becoming the vendor of choice in any industry.

Michael introduced me to a simple, yet powerful formula many years ago; and the understanding of this formula changed my professional career forever. Not only was I able to achieve my sales quotas, but also suddenly I became a true rainmaker.

We have already analyzed how the value we place on the product or service we are acquiring dictates our buying criteria. We have learned that this value is both relative and subjective, and we have realized that we all perceive value differently. Essentially, we all expect to receive some form of value when we buy something. Rarely will we buy a product or service if the perceived value is equal or less than zero.

Michael calls this *Expected Value* (EV), or the minimum benefit we expect to receive from the product or service we are buying. In our roles as business developers or as project managers, while leveraging our time in front of customers, expected value alone is not enough to differentiate us from the competition. When presented with multiple alternatives, a customer or prospective buyer needs to make and justify a purchasing decision. The customer will select the professional that succeeds at differentiating his or her products or services better than the competition.

Only those that are capable of <u>increasing</u> the *perceived value* of what they are selling will start to separate themselves from the competition. Michael Vickers describes this effort in his book as *"up-leveling"* and represents it by the **Distinctive Value** (DV) element in his formula. What is it that you and only you (or your product or company) can do differently to separate you from the pack?

This is of particular importance in the competitive world of commodity selling, for many products and services that were once leading edge innovations (high value), are now simple commodities (low value). Examples are abundant in our daily lives: Cell phones and cell phone services, cable and satellite TV services, airline carriers, electronic organizers, personal computers, etc.

When an innovation becomes readily available in the marketplace it starts to commoditize, hence, it naturally loses value and it opens the door for a competing vendor to innovate again and demand a higher price for the same product or service, and so the cycle repeats itself multiple times.

In a marketplace crowded with multiple vendors, offering the same product or service (commodity) it is increasingly more difficult to differentiate from the competition. Some do it through attractive packaging, others by offering gifts, or by lowering price. Commoditization gave way to the loyalty reward systems we know today.

The only way to separate one credit card company from another was by allowing consumers to collect points, who could then redeem them for merchandise or services; and so the loyalty program was born. What was then an innovative strategy to capture and retain customers it is now an expected element in the credit card industry, a commodity service.

The only problem with Distinctive Value is that it is very short-lived. What is distinctive today becomes the norm tomorrow. Who can succeed in this environment then? —Only those who can consistently find creative ways of differentiating themselves from the competition will survive in a highly commoditized marketplace.

We have already mentioned the case of Apple. The almost yearly releases of their music players, smart phones, and now tablets, are perfect examples of what continuous innovation is all about. This tactic, coupled with an effective marketing and branding strategy is what has rewarded the Cupertino-based company with the loyalty (and advocacy) levels we observe today.

Distinctive people

Often products, services, or even companies do not make the difference. In many cases, the people involved in the value-creating chain can have such an impact on the customer experience that their own behavior can easily make the difference.

Earlier in my career, I was a project manager with a technology company in Calgary, Canada. This city nested in the oil producing Province of Alberta is a short drive away from the breath-taking views of the Rocky Mountains and the beautiful town of Banff. When my customer was due to attend project meetings in Calgary, he decided to bring his wife and newborn child to visit Canada for the first time.

As a project manager, I was playing host and immediately felt compelled to make them feel welcomed in the city. I took them to various restaurants, showed them a good time in town, drove them to the mountains, etc. One morning my client told me he was very concerned with his baby boy, who became sick overnight and was quickly deteriorating.

He was in meetings, stranded with my team in the office, and his wife did not speak English very well and was alone at the hotel with the baby. I immediately called my wife and asked her to call my client's spouse and find out what the situation was. I told my customer to relax and wait a few minutes to hear back from my wife. Five minutes later, she called and explained she would try to get them to see our pediatrician, and if not possible, she would drive them to the emergency room, as most likely the baby in severe dehydration from the nightlong ordeal.

Our pediatrician was kind enough to accommodate an unscheduled visit to his office. After examining the baby, he was able to determine he had the flu; he then prescribed adequate medication and treatment, and sent the boy home. My client (and his wife) perceived this simple little effort on my wife's part as a huge demonstration of kindness, considering they were in a foreign country, not able to understand the language, and not knowing what to do. Not only was he thankful for what we did at the time, but through the experience we also became friends for life. More importantly, the experience helped removed any barriers of trust that existed prior to these events and our project moved smoothly and ended up being a complete success.

Distinctive Value can be delivered in many different ways and by whom you least expect.

The importance of *trust*

The multiplier in this equation is **Trust** (T), which means that only by building significant amounts of trust between you and your customer or prospective buyer is that you will be able to put this formula into practice. Without trust, your efforts for delivering Distinctive Value will be a waste. This is where differentiation really takes off. Once trust is built between you and your customer, then the doors are open to execute your selling strategy (need creation, need justification, consultative, ROI-based selling, etc.).

In my opinion, trust is the number one barrier to securing business—especially repeat-business. Once a customer buys from you, your company has only one chance to make and keep that customer happy. The client *expects* certain *value* in return and it is your organization's job to *up-level* the delivery of your product or service, so the customer can start to appreciate the existence of something unique, something that no other vendor would be able to deliver, the existence of something truly *distinctive*.

If your organization succeeds in delivering *distinctive value*, while at the same time building a significant amount of *trust* between the two parties, only then you are ready to attempt what is perhaps the most difficult task in sales: Obtaining **Repeat Business**. This is when an existing customer decides to come back and buy more of the same or a different product or service from you and your organization. Achieving this is what Michael refers to in his book as **Preferred Status**.

So, in the formula EV + DV * T = PS, the desired outcome is *Preferred Status*, which is obtained by delivering what is expected from us as a minimum (*Expected Value*), together with a whole new experience, an improvement over what the norm is (*Distinctive Value*); and by coupling that with massive amounts of *Trust*. We covered trust-building examples in previous chapters, but of course, honesty and the highest integrity standards are also excellent ways for building trust.

Chapter 9

Frozen Food

If you go back and read the previous chapter again, you will realize we just wrote the chapter on *Customer Satisfaction*. A satisfied customer is no other than the one that was impressed not only by the quality of the product or service we delivered, but also by how different the whole experience was from everything else he or she had experienced before. In addition, a satisfied customer is one that recognizes he/she felt at ease when doing business with you and your company.

When do we feel at ease when doing business with others? – When we feel that we are being treated with respect, honesty, and integrity; when we feel we are important, when our problems are being resolved, when the vendor is extremely competent in the field we are concerned with, when we are learning from the supplier, and when we grow our knowledge and expertise in the discipline or technology being utilized. That is when we feel most comfortable, and a customer that feels at ease when making a purchasing decision is already destined to becoming a satisfied customer, unless the company providing the product, project, or service really does a terrible job and destroys what was built before. This is one of the key messages behind this book.

In my personal opinion, customer satisfaction is going through a crisis, not only in the United States, but also throughout the world. All you have to do to realize this is call any of your personal suppliers (credit card company, utility company, cellular service company, health care provider, cable or satellite vendor, airline company, etc.), or go to any store in your city, and simply ask for help in resolving an issue with the quality of the service you are receiving.

Thousands of companies around the world spend billions of dollars every year in an effort to improve customer satisfaction; and the results are less than impressive. The most conservative studies show that consumers are not satisfied at all with the quality of service we receive and that we are in a continuous search for a better provider for virtually every product and service we buy.

This (social) phenomenon intrigues me deeply. Why do companies spend so much money on expert consultants to help them improve their customer experience, and yet the indicators show that customer satisfaction is in a continuous decline? In fact, it has been in a nosedive for the last three decades!

To me customer satisfaction (or customer success, as I prefer to call it) is like frozen food. It must remain at a constant low temperature to ensure it stays fresh. It is very easy to break this *cold-chain* during product transportation from the manufacturing plant to the distribution warehouse, and from the warehouse to the point of sale. If the temperature in the trucks is higher than it should be, it will damage the products, and no matter how much effort everybody else had put into keeping a steady low temperature everywhere else, the result will be a bad product, always.

The same occurs with customer satisfaction. It only takes one person to ruin the efforts of many and the millions of dollars invested to ensure the complete customer experience chain works flawlessly. One little mistake and all efforts are in vain. Dissatisfied customers not only will never come back, but what is worse, unhappy clients will never *advocate* for us.

A melting experience

Speaking of low temperatures let me share with you a personal experience with a bad service and how the company's reaction to solving my problem only came to reaffirm they did not effectively understand customer success or their business:

It was the hot summer of 2011 in Houston, Texas. I was on a business trip in Europe and I was destined to miss our wedding anniversary. Although I could not be there in person, I wanted to make sure my wife knew I did not forget such an important date. What do men do when faced with such a puzzling dilemma? —We take advantage of 21st Century technology and order flowers online.

I selected a beautiful bouquet of two-dozen impeccable red roses and to ensure I had guaranteed forgiveness for not being home to celebrate the event in person, I added some chocolates in a heart-shaped box. I made sure my order included guaranteed delivery on the exact date of our anniversary. If you have ever forgotten your wedding anniversary day, you know there was a lot at stake for me then, and money was not an issue when it came to checking out and entering my credit card number on the computer (willingness to pay).

The important day came and as soon as I received the email confirming delivery was successful, I called my wife and I said with proud tone:

- *"Happy Anniversary my dear! Did you like the flowers I sent...?"*

To my amazement her response was:

- *"Well, I'm sure they were once very beautiful..."*

Not only had the flowers withered during transportation, but also the chocolates had melted. I quickly called the company and complained about the situation, demanding an immediate solution. I did not believe my ears when they immediately offered to resend the order with next day guaranteed delivery, free of charge. *"Wow, what a service!"* I thought.

Sure enough, the next day I got the confirmation email indicating delivery was complete, and so I proceeded to call my wife again. She said:

- *"You will not believe this, but the new flowers and chocolates arrived in exactly the same condition as yesterday."*

It was not a laughable matter, so I called them again and this time I asked:

- *"Could you tell me where you are shipping the flowers from?"*

- *"We ship our flowers out of New York sir."*

- *"Could you tell me what shipping method you are using for sending flowers to your customers in Texas?"* (This was an actual call with a nationwide, well-recognized flower delivery company). The customer representative's answer was:

- *"Well sir, we use any of the major US land and air carriers."*

When I asked if they used refrigerated or air-conditioned trucks, she said that they did not and that it was not necessary.

- *"Do you realize it is 104 degrees in Houston right now?"* (This is equivalent to $40°$ C, for those of you—like me—used to the metric system).

She did not know what to say. My tone changed from astonishment to frustration and the following dialogue took place over the phone line:

- *"How much extra do I need to pay for you to deliver the flowers in an air-conditioned truck?"*

- *"Sir, as I said before, we do not use air-conditioned trucks."*

- *"I understand, but my question was different. How much extra is it going to cost me to have you guys figure out a way to put the flowers in an air-conditioned truck?"*

- *"Sorry sir, we cannot do it."*

I was prepared (and willing) to pay anything to make this happen and yet they were not interested in understanding the root of the problem, or in solving it. How can a nationwide flower delivery company do business without understanding that the temperatures in New York are very different from those in Texas, and that flowers (and chocolates) have a tendency to die under extremely high temperatures?

Perhaps I was expecting too much from a big name business, or perhaps my demands were unreasonable, but I was not prepared to give up. I called my neighborhood flower store and explained my ordeal. Not only did the owner have what I wanted, but had delivery service as well. Her store was only five minutes away from the house and the bill was 25% lower than the big online store.

Now, what do you think...?

- Would I have paid the same price for this service? –Of course!
- Would I have paid a premium for this simple but effective service? –Happily!
- Would I buy again from the big name online store? – Obviously not!
- Even in winter? –Never!

Here lies the true problem behind this story: Dissatisfied customers will never come back, even if the situation is different (like if temperatures are lower in this case). In fact, I am sure that if they called me today announcing they have started using refrigerated or air-conditioned trucks for deliveries, I would still not go back.

Selling a product or service is very much like going to a job interview. You have only five minutes to cause a good first impression. Nothing you do after those five minutes will ever change that first impression. They may change their opinion overall, and even hire you, but the image of the first impression will always be there.

Businesses have a very small window of opportunity to *wow* their customers. If they fail at delivering an excellent customer experience the first time around, seldom will they get a second chance.

With today's technology and access to the Internet and social networks, it is very easy for anybody to damage a company's reputation. It only takes a few seconds for anybody to search for a company name online and dozens of websites offering reviews of their products and services fill our computer screen. Rarely have I encountered a company without mistakes, complaints, or frustrated customers.

Nevertheless, a very inconspicuous (social) phenomenon takes place here. People tend to go through the trouble of writing a review only when their experience with a product or service has been bad. It seems to be less frequent for people to take the time to write a review when everything went perfectly. This skews the trend somewhat and consumers should remain aware of this statistical error when selecting a product or service provider, based purely on consumer reviews.

I am very passionate about this subject, and one can write a complete book about it. The important point here is to realize and embrace the power of a simple little formula, $EV + DV * T = PS$. Thanks Mike!

Chapter 10

Advocacy

Nothing facilitates repeat business more than having satisfied, loyal customers; and nothing can erode your revenue stream more easily than having upset, dissatisfied clients. However, in order for a business to grow, it also needs new customers and new projects, and here is where your existing clients can help you by advocating for your products and services.

In the case of the swimming pool construction project example, would you recommend Company-C to all your friends and relatives wanting to build a pool? –Enthusiastically, I am sure. More importantly, you will tell them to make sure they get the same project manager you had assigned to your project.

Only Company-C was capable of delivering value beyond all expectations, and with similar effort to that of his competitors the PM was able to secure the business for his company during the first meeting. Was Company-C any better at building pools than the other bidders? –Most likely not. Will you ever be able to tell if any of the other two contractors would have been as good (or better) in building your pool? –Probably not.

This example taught us several lessons, like the importance of putting the right people in front of the customer at the right time (*Time & Event*), or the power of educating your customer with useful information. We also learned about the magic effects of not talking about our products or company in the first meeting, and focus on learning about the customer and his or her frustrations, wishes, and desires instead.

This example also taught us how much customers value perceptions, to the point of being willing to entrust the construction of their project to a company based purely on the good impression the company's representative caused in the first meeting. If the project was successful once completed, then you have a customer for life, and unless something goes terribly wrong later on (*Frozen Food*), no competitor will be able to drive that customer away.

Perhaps the swimming pool case is not ideal to exemplify how customers return for more, time after time; but if you take this example to another kind of project, like a hair salon, a computer repair shop, or a car maintenance place, you will start to see the effect. Now take this to the reality of the corporate world where customers actually do buy more than one project and you will appreciate the power of advocacy.

The energy sector is a good example. Power transmission companies execute multiple projects a year to extend their reach. Oil & Gas transportation companies build pipelines every year to take their products to new markets or processing facilities. Exploration & Production companies drill new wells in search of new crude oil, etc. All this activity generates multiple projects, the perfect place for repeat-business and advocacy.

Satisfied customers not only will return with more projects and ask for you and your team, but they will also refer your company to their friends, so more prospective buyers will call asking for quotes.

Most project-driven companies struggle to deliver successful projects to their customers (the way the customer defines success), and therefore cannot grow. They respond by simply adding more salespeople with impressive *Rolodexes*, only to see the cycle repeat itself. Effective companies thrive by consistently delivering successful projects (the way the customer defines success) that create extremely satisfied customers willing to advocate for their business and their people.

Here lies the true power of the PM in creating advocating behavior from existing clients. Our project teams should be concerned with wowing customers every day. It goes back again to the exceeding expectations concept. Every time we impress our customers, we are creating a loyal customer, one that is not only willing to return for more, but also to recommend our company, products, services, and team members to others.

Sales teams can promise a hundred times that the next project will be better. Your CEO can sign in blood that next time will be different; but never securing an order has been as easy as to when we are dealing with a satisfied customer, or with a new client that came recommended to our company and our people by one of our satisfied customers.

In conclusion, the key to repeat business and new customers does not lie in hiring a new sales manager with an impressive *Rolodex*, but in having absolutely satisfied customers, so they can come back for more, and later advocate for us.

Success

The role of the PM and project team is then to ensure all projects are extremely successful, not only for their own company, but also for the client's organization. This is perhaps the most difficult challenge, because often what is a successful project for your company means a not very happy customer, and vice versa.

Think about it for a moment, for your company a successful project is one that delivered a profitable bottom line. The project could have taken twice as long to execute, but if you were able to squeeze enough change orders from your customer, most likely you were able to deliver a profitable result to your company, and therefore have a good reason to celebrate, right?

Now, look at this same scenario from your client's eyes. From their perspective their project is not only late (which had an impact on their own ability to generate revenues), but it cost them far more than what was contractually agreed with your company.

In their opinion, you, your team, and your company failed to deliver on their basic expectation. What is worse, the extra revenue you were able to capture for your company to help compensate for the overruns and keep the project's bottom line from turning red has left a bitter taste in your client's mouth.

- Does the customer have a reason to celebrate?
- Will they consider your company for their next project?
- Will they recommend your organization to others?

The answers to these questions are obvious, so the next time your boss asks if your project is going to be successful, your answer should always be *"it depends."* Yes, it depends on who is evaluating success. Is it your own organization or your client's company? A true successful project is the one that delivers a successful result to both sides of the table. Now, that would be reason for celebration!

Chapter 11

Leverage

Leverage truly is a social tool that is widely used in business, not only by executives and sales professionals, but also by many other individuals. PMs, for example, use it regularly to tilt the scale to their side when dealing with deviations, non-conformances, delays, penalties, or change orders. Relationship leverage is only one dimension of this tool; however it is the one that first comes to mind when we think about leverage in business.

However, leverage can take many other forms, beyond the obvious. In our *Need Creation* examples, we analyzed how to deliver *Value* by educating a client about how to use your products or services to solve their problems. There we were applying leverage to our advantage. By giving something away (the value of knowledge) we are building an image of expertise around our company (*Trust*), which in turn plays a pivotal role when it comes to purchasing decisions.

If we do not do it, somebody else will; and whoever does it first has the advantage (lever) to generate revenue from this particular client. It is very simple, but very powerful at the same time. The strange thing is that salespeople know about this and would love to use it all the time, but often they cannot. Either they lack the expert technical knowledge about a particular product, or they fail at engaging the customer appropriately, simply because they forgot the importance of *Trust*. Yes, selling is the salespeople's job, however sometimes it is not the right time for them to be in front of the customer (*Time & Event*).

Technical people—and project managers in particular—can seamlessly appear before potential buyers and tell a story, without making it obvious that the ultimate objective is to build trust, influence their minds, and later *leverage* that feeling to trigger a purchasing decision. Here lies the importance of having PMs and salespeople reading this book at the same time. Business development is a strategy, perhaps the most important of all corporate strategies, and as such, all stakeholders in the organization should plan and implement it jointly. Remember, we are in the business of <u>making money</u>.

Now, let us analyze the more pejorative classification of leverage: ***Relationship Leverage***. Often people confuse this kind of leverage with some form of corruption—big mistake! Leverage and corruption are two completely different things. One of the most valuable assets any human being can posses is the relationship with others. People develop relationships at different levels, including friendship. Some even argue there are different levels of friendship too, but that is subject of a different, more philosophical discussion.

The truth is that meeting someone is one of the simplest most beautiful events a person can experience. It can be a casual introduction or a more formal event that brings two individuals together. Regardless, how deep that relationship will go only depends on those two individuals. Many dimensions of psychology (including personality) play a role in how relationships develop, which is a completely different topic I invite you to explore on your own.

Introverts may have a more difficult time meeting new people, whilst extroverts may go about introducing themselves in a crowd as a fairly normal (and expected) behavior. Nonetheless, the truth to the matter is that no matter what, we are social people; we are genetically programmed to function among other people. Very few individuals have managed to be successful in isolation. Being timid is not a defect or a disadvantage; to the contrary, conservative studies show that introverts are better at performing tasks that demand high levels of concentration, like writing computer code, for example.

Extroverts, on the other hand, have tremendous difficulty remaining focused on a single task. They cannot help themselves but need to get up and interact, make a phone call, or simply shift their minds into multiple issues at once.

No matter what your personality trait is, I encourage you to invest time in developing your personal relationships. Networking with peers, superiors, and subordinates alike is a good start. Expanding our network of contacts beyond our inner circle is the next step. The broader the network, the more our own knowledge grows, and the more leverage opportunities we have at our disposal.

Need a new dentist? —Ask your friends and acquaintances to recommend one. Lost your job? —Let everybody know you are looking for a new opportunity, they will keep their eyes and ears open for you. Need a customer referral? —Ask colleagues in your field to help you open doors. Need an introduction to a decision maker? —Ask your network of contacts and they will put you in contact with the right individual.

Leverage your relationships and the results will astonish you.

Can you think of other types of leverage? There is *situational leverage*, for example. Let us go back to our swimming pool construction project case. There, the homeowners had a dream (*wish or desire*): To have a pool in their backyard. Which contractor completely ignored those feelings (*the situation*) and proceeded almost robotically to execute a sales script? —You are correct, the first two vendors did.

Company-C's representative was the only one who took time to observe the feelings in the home owners and in doing so realized he could _leverage_ the situation to transform those feelings into *need*, while at the same time positioning himself and his company as the *preferred* contractor by educating the customer about the pool construction process, and therefore building *trust*.

In my career, I have seen many corporations struggling to identify leverage opportunities and use them appropriately. I must insist on the *Time & Event* principle we covered earlier. Only the right individual, at the right time and at the right place should use leverage, as is the case with any other tactic. This is why it is so important for project managers and technical people in general to be part of business development strategies. Again, often salespeople are <u>not</u> the right individuals to be in front of the customer, given the circumstances.

Leverage opportunities are everywhere around us, we just need to learn how to identify them and quickly create a tactic to capitalize on them and use them to tilt the scale and start generating revenue. Leverage should be present in our minds every day, reminding us that every action we take (or decide not to take) will always have an impact on our ability to use leverage in the future.

When you decide not to attend that event you were invited to, you are renouncing to the opportunity of meeting new people and growing your network of contacts, and in doing so, you are perhaps missing on a valuable opportunity to use leverage sometime in the near or distant future.

When somebody asks you for a favor and you decline, you are negating the possibility of leveraging that situation in the future. Often people do not even ask for favors, they simply need help. You should always be ready to lend a helping hand, you will gain a friend for life, and before you know it, that person will be ready to reciprocate when you need it most.

Chapter 12

Push vs. Pull Theory

Pushing is a natural behavior. We all have a tendency to try to convince others of our points of view, or to follow our actions or beliefs. We have observed this behavior even in our teen years. Do you remember your first date, or your first boyfriend/girlfriend? Can you remember how you felt after your first breakup?

Most likely, you quickly reacted and tried to convince your partner that he or she was making a big mistake by ending the relationship. Your friends told you to take the back seat, be cool, and wait patiently for the other to return and make up; but instead you chased after what you believed was right and you used every argument in your repertoire to try to convince the other person of your viewpoint, right?

Why is it so difficult for us to take a more passive approach when we are so clearly convinced of what needs to be done? Why is it in our nature to open the toolbox and start pulling whatever resources we have at our disposal to achieve our objectives?

If you analyze a company's typical customer meeting ritual, you will almost certainly observe the same *push* behavior most of the time:

Salespeople (often too many at a time) walk into the meeting room, perform introductions, exchange business cards, open their briefcases, ask for a projector, pull a laptop computer out, hook everything up, and like robots start talking to a series of standard slides with great enthusiasm and professionalism.

Typically, the slideshow will cover general corporate aspects first, in an attempt to convince the client that the company is the best, the largest, or the first at pretty much everything:

- *"We are the number one supplier of..."*
- *"We are the largest company in..."*
- *"Our product is the best at..."*

Also the concept of being *"worldwide"* usually appears somewhere in those lines too. If every corporation is the best, the largest, or the first in the world, then where are all the other companies? Not only this approach lacks humility, but also it is naive at the same time. What is worse, (and trust me on this) our customers are getting tired of it.

After 30 minutes or so of corporate slide talk, they move onto describing their company products and/or services. Dozens of busy slides occupy the large screen with the sole purpose of convincing the client that the company's products or services are the best in the world. The client asks a few questions, mainly because they feel sorry for the poor salesperson that just managed to put his audience to sleep, and literally insulted them with such a cliché presentation. Somebody once called this scenario *"death by PowerPoint."*

The client had given the salesperson one hour maximum for the meeting. With 30 minutes into overtime, he finally gets to the *"Thanks for your attention!"* slide, followed by the obvious *"Do you have any questions?"* At that point, the client looks at the time and says *"No, excellent presentation. Thanks for coming..."*

What did just happen here?

Did we learn anything about the customer or their project(s) during this meeting?

This is a very common example of a *Push* sales tactic, not very different from what Company-A and Company-B did in our pool construction case. Our natural instinct when selling anything is to push and in doing so try to convince our audience that our widget is better than the competition's. Everybody does it, so we think this is the right thing to do and what customers expect. We do not realize that they hate it and get frustrated with typical *push* performances, time after time.

Remember my client who travelled to Canada with his wife and newborn son? He now works for a well-respected oil services company, and as such, he now sits on the other side of the table. Now he needs to face different customers everyday and knows exactly how they feel when a typical *elevator pitch* is pulled out of a hat, like a magician pulls out a rabbit.

Pulling

A *Pull* tactic, by contrast, looks completely different and it usually works significantly better. *Pushing* seems to be only about <u>us</u>, while *Pulling* is all about the <u>customer</u>. A good *Pull* tactic usually means:

- Taking control
- Listening
- Getting as much information as you can
- Avoid talking about your company, products, or services.

Every time a client grants us a meeting, we want to take a protagonist role by standing in front of the audience and driving our sales pitch. It takes a significant amount of courage and maturity to take the backseat instead, and as Company-C's project manager did in our pool construction example, keep our company and product material in the briefcase.

It is so difficult already to get access to our clients and prospective buyers, that it seems so wrong to waste that small window of opportunity by doing all the talking. We want to learn about <u>them</u> as much as we can; about their stress, about what keeps them awake at night, and about their problems and challenges. Therefore, we need to ask smart questions and have them talking, not the other way around!

After years of analyzing this problem in real-life scenarios, I have concluded that typically salespeople have a natural tendency to *push*, while PMs tend to *pull*. Furthermore, PMs generally do not feel comfortable *pushing* at all, while salespeople cannot help themselves but to *push*.

The following are some situations I have generally observed over the years:

1. Customers do not like it when we *push*.
2. Salespeople do not know how to *pull*.
3. When they do, they do not have the client's *trust*, so they fail.
4. PMs hate to *push* and are natural *pullers*.

What can we conclude from these observations? —Companies should unleash their project managers and let them *pull* all they want!

An ideal *pull* sales meeting should be all about the customer and not so much about you, your company, or your product. The best way to set the stage for such a meeting is not to have a slide presentation at all, and if you must use slides, they should simply describe your understanding of the customer and the business opportunity or project.

You should use those assumptions to ask verification questions as you talk:

*   *"I understand your company is headquartered in Boston and employs about 1,500 people, correct?"*
*   *"My understanding is that you plan to start a tender process to build a new natural gas pipeline in your region, and that your bid deadline is March 10th. Is that correct?"*

- *"I was told that you have a budget of $55 million dollars for this project. Is my information accurate?"*
- *"What characteristics are important to you when looking for the ideal company to build your project?"*
- *"Are you contracting directly, or through a third party?"*
- *"How much do you know about our company, our subject matter experts, and our products/solutions?"*
- *"Who are the key members of your project team?"*
- *"Can you share an organization chart of your project team with me?"*
- *"When do you plan on awarding this contract?"*
- *"Do you have any questions for me?"*
- *"When could we meet again?"*

This last question is perhaps the most important of them all. A supporter will always be willing to meet you again, while an opponent will always find reasons not to receive you. Pay special attention to this aspect.

Letting your prospective buyers know about your company, products, and services is a *Marketing* function, not *Sales*. Nor is it part of *Project Execution*. If you find yourself having to introduce your company or products to the customer, that means that your marketing is poor, and you should challenge your employer to improve their marketing strategy.

A pull selling approach is about putting the customer in the center of the universe and keeping your company, its products, and services in your briefcase.

Chapter 13

PMs & The Three Business Development Models

There are typically three main business development models or approaches, which are based on the relationship between four key elements:

1. Market
2. Products
3. Customers
4. Orders

And three key functions:
1. Sales
2. Marketing
3. Service

The *Market* is the playfield where the entire magic takes place, as *Customers* (and their demand) get together with vendors (and their supply). Using *Sales* and *Marketing* functions, vendors do their best to get *Orders* for their *Products* or *Services*.

Some may argue that this is only true in a free market economy environment. In theory, this is correct, but in reality, the supply and demand equation is applicable even in the most radical of the economies.

I have been blessed with the opportunity to visit many countries and have even lived in several different places; and I have witnessed several economic models first hand. I believe I speak with a certain degree of authority when I say with conviction that supply and demand-based trading, including willingness to pay pricing theory, applies in all types of economic environments.

Even in the extreme economic model of a communist country, I witnessed supply and demand forces that drove prices in one direction or another. If the government tried to stop inflation by setting the price of basic goods, like chicken, milk, or eggs below the cost of production, private companies will have no option but to reduce production and sell in a parallel (black) market. The regulation caused product shortages, and consumers suddenly were *willing* to pay 400% the original price to obtain what they needed. Willingness to pay and Supply and demand do apply even in the extreme of a communist economy.

Let us go back to our topic and analyze the most typical model, the Product-Centric Business Development Approach:

Product-Centric Model

Here, the center of the universe is the product or widget and the customer and market take a secondary role. Our product is the star and everything else revolves around it, and deserves minimal attention. Our sales strategy is incomplete, for our understanding of the marketplace and the customer is poor. Our marketing execution is often misaligned with reality.

Product-driven selling models are often present in companies that once produced a leading-edge product that the market embraced enthusiastically. As competition moved-in, and innovation quickly turned to commodity, ego got in the way and the company failed to follow its customers and the marketplace signs. Furthermore, it failed at understanding its competitors.

The company believed so strongly in its products that it invested heavily in taking them in the wrong direction, ignoring customer needs (and desires), and what everybody else was doing. Some may argue that simply following what others are doing inhibits innovation. However, when customers are clearly telling us that what we are building is not what they want or need, sometimes it is wise to listen. Do you remember the evolution of handheld devices?

Salespeople performing at this level spend most of their customer-facing time talking about their product, trying to convince their audience that their widget is better than the competition's. Their slide show presentations are repetitive, vertical, and promote one-way communication.

Next, we have the Market-Centric Business Development Approach. Here the product takes the backseat, giving way to the market as the centerpiece. We have a good understanding of the marketplace, our customers' needs, our competitors, and their products. We have a clear idea of price brackets and barriers to entry. We know the niche size for our widgets and can make safe growth projections.

Market-Centric Model

Here, our customer meeting opportunities revolve around finding out more about the client's needs, desires, and motivations. We spend considerable time understanding their vendor-selection process and mapping their organization structure well. We know who the decision makers and influencers are, and we carefully design a strategy that tackles them both at the same time.

Our corporation carefully plans its product development based on market signs. We understand what our competitors are doing and we know what our customer's problems and frustrations are. Our main objective is to serve the market with a combination of own and third party products.

Lastly, we have the Customer-Centric Business Development Model. In this case, the customer is right in the middle and all elements and functions revolve around the client. Our sole objective is to get orders from our customer, and for that, we utilize everything we know about selling, including what we have learned in this book.

Not only do we have a deep understanding of the marketplace, but also we have challenged our company to improve its marketing strategies (including product direction and branding) to facilitate our market penetration efforts. As a consequence our widgets are well known for the quality and advanced features they possess, and our brand enjoys high recognition and association with the market segment we are serving.

Our project execution and customer service functions are outstanding and our relationship with the client base and prospective buyers cannot be better. We fully understand our customers' structure, we know who the decision makers, influencers, and evaluators are in the organization, and key members of our team have strong _Trust_ relationships with all of them.

We know the customer's industry, their challenges, their frustrations, and their dreams. We are fully aware of their future strategic investment plans and we know exactly what they liked and did not like about previous vendors. In other words, we have an intimate understanding of the client.

Customer-Centric Model

By putting the customer first, we also succeed in paying attention to both the market and our product offering as well, as our client base is the main source of ideas for our product direction. Not only do we have a close relationship with our existing customers, but also a deep understanding of our potential clients. We know exactly why they are buying our competitor's widgets and not ours.

We cannot see the forest for the trees

I do not believe there is an ideal selling model, or that one is better than the other is. My opinion is that achieving our company's ultimate business goal (to make money) is no easy task. Often we see a simplistic approach to growing a company's market share and more often than necessary, we observe companies of all sizes focusing too narrowly on one model over another.

What is the natural reaction when sales are down? —Companies hire more salespeople.

What do companies do to hurt their competitors' order intake? —They lure competitors' best salespeople to join the company.

This behavior is typical of product-centric selling tactics. Companies are so obscured by declining sales that they fail to see that the sales function is not the problem!

We can tell potential clients that our products are better than those they are buying today as much as we want. We can say it every day, in many different languages, but rarely customers change their minds simply because of our insistence. We can throw a different salesperson at them every week and nothing will happen.

It is all about *market erosion*. Think about it for a minute: We are all in business trying either to erode our competitor's market position, or to protect ours, which means of course that our competitors are also trying to erode our own market share position and defend theirs. In the end, it is all about a market-erosion game.

If this theory is correct, then why do so many companies insist on downplaying the role of the *marketing* function and the important role of non-salespeople in the business generation equation? If the goal is to grow our market share position, companies should adopt a more holistic approach to business development. Product-centric models tend to ignore the market and neglect the customer and therefore are destined to fail, or as a minimum to have a short-lived success.

We are part of a highly dynamic business world and everything we do to improve our results has an effect on what others are doing. We should never ignore this cause and effect phenomenon when planning the company's next market penetration strategy. No matter how brilliant our plan or how grandiose our results, they will always change, for the other forces in this dynamic business environment are not dormant and are always alert to react to our actions.

Not a single enterprise has ever been able to sustain an ever-growing business model. Perhaps many have succeeded in growing for many years, but even the biggest of empires eventually crumbles down to give way to the competitor that knew how to recognize the mistakes that often come with being at the top.

A business leader once told me: *"It's not fun to be number one. Getting to this place was the easy part. Staying here is proving to be more challenging than I thought."*

Companies that are winning the market erosion battle face a difficult challenge to stay there. It is a lonely place up there, as everybody else is putting significant effort into taking that position. Often the biggest breakthroughs in innovation come from companies fiercely fighting for market share and not from those at the top.

Neglecting the customer is perhaps the biggest mistake a company can make; therefore implementing a customer-centric strategy usually pays higher dividends than a product-centric approach alone. A weak understanding of the marketplace and our competitors is another big mistake. In addition, building the wrong product will assure declining sales.

In my opinion, a combination of business development models is the key to success. Think of it as a cocktail recipe: A perfect drink is the result of a perfect balance between its ingredients. All three selling models are important and have a role in helping our companies succeed in their quest for growth. The key is to know how much of each model should go in the blender.

Now, who is closest to the customer? Who is out in the field interacting with the end users of the products and services your company sells? Who is best positioned to have a true intimate understanding of the marketplace and customers? –You guessed it, project managers, and the technical experts that work tirelessly to deliver a successful project to the client are in the ideal position to make a massive contribution to the success of the business development strategy of your corporation.

This is why I wrote this book, not to turn project managers into salespeople, but to show them how they can dramatically further their careers by playing a pivotal role in the continued success of their organizations.

Chapter 14

Checkmate

Life is a strategic game. We carefully analyze every decision we have to make, weighing every alternative, considering the advantages and disadvantages of every possibility. We often draw a mental map of our options and determine the future benefits and dangers of each one before making a final decision. In essence, we are drawing a chessboard in our minds and playing with every possible move before committing to the one we think is the best move possible.

The business world is not so different. Project managers face difficult decisions on a daily basis, such as:

- *"Should I send this letter to the customer now, or should I wait a little longer?"*
- *"Should I charge the customer for this little extra work, or is it better to just throw it in and use it as leverage later?"*
- *"Should I document the fact that the customer was two weeks late in approving the design or should I let it go and do not bother?"*

Such are typical situations PMs often encounter in their daily jobs. Even complex algorithmic decision trees exist to deal with more difficult business decisions. In the end, a chessboard—or more precisely, the game of chess—can help represent every decision.

Early in my career, one of my mentors once told me that playing golf was not a sport, but a business skill. He was right, as most business people like to play golf, and more importantly, discuss business matters while approaching the green.

I personally think that chess is also a business skill, perhaps more so than golf. Have you realized that managing projects is a little like being at war? You are always accumulating evidence either to defend yourself from an attack from your customers, or to claim something from them.

The client-vendor relationship should always start on a solid foundation of trust, but even in the best of cases, both sides are always weighing the effects of every move, guessing the cause and effect of every decision.

In the game of chess, every move has the potential of getting you one step closer to winning, or one step closer to losing the game. Therefore, players must carefully study and plan every single move. Your ability to get into your opponent's mind and guess what his or her next move might be in reaction to yours is what differentiates a good chess player from an average one.

Experts say that the best chess player is not the one that makes the best moves, but the one that knows exactly how the opponent will react to every move. That is the key to winning at this game, and so it is in business.

Chess players are constantly building decision trees in their heads, carefully analyzing every possible move and their corresponding reaction from the opponent. Business leaders and salespeople practice the same strategy and project managers are not very different, for the art and science of managing projects always involves dealing with customers under tough contractual conditions, which means everything we do as PMs can be used against us, our team, and our company.

The art of playing chess is an essential skill in business. All professional project managers, salespeople, and business leaders alike should learn this game, practice it, mastered it, and apply it in the corporate world.

An experienced entrepreneur once told me: *"The best business decision is the one you make tomorrow."* This is a very deep concept! Seriously, postponing a tough decision until we cool-off is perhaps one of the best tactics anyone can implement in business or personal life. No good comes out of tough decisions made on the spot, while the issue is still hot.

So next time you are faced with a tough decision, put the issue on ice, walk away from it completely, and do not do anything until the next day. Write a draft email if you must, but by no means send it. I promise you the next day it will sound completely different, and nine out of ten times, you will end up deleting it or re-writing it in a softer, more conciliating tone.

It helps to build a decision tree in your head or draw it on a piece of paper. Then think of a chess game and carefully evaluate every possible move. This is very important not only during sale cycles, but also during project execution. We already learned that good project delivery, together with trust lead the way to repeat business.

In a competitive business environment, such as a tender process for example, the game of chess takes on a completely new meaning. Multiple bidders are competing for the same piece of business on a leveled playfield. The rules are usually clear and conditions are equal for all participants.

During proposal preparation, all bidders are defining their strategies, which also involve guessing what the others are doing. Sometimes one participant will send deceiving or distracting messages by making an unexpected move. Guessing how our opponents will react to our every move is the key to gaining an edge in this type of scenarios.

There are many lessons to learn from the game of chess in this regard. I encourage you to learn it, play it, and master the skill of carefully analyzing your every move, as well as your opponent's reactions.

Chapter 15

The Art of War*

Chess is in simple terms a war game. Your army's job is to defend your kingdom and attack the enemy. You must revise your initial strategy with every move. You sacrifice some soldiers in order to protect your king and queen and to get closer to invading your enemy's territory. Each player tries to position his or her pieces strategically in preparation for the right moment to attack.

Your job is to guess what the opponent's strategy is and block their next move before it happens, so they have to change their plan constantly, weakening their chances of success. Each piece has a specific role and limitations in what it can do; some are more powerful in their offensive reach, while others are more effective in defending the kingdom.

More than 2,000 years ago Sun Tzu, a Chinese army general wrote a book entitled *The Art of War*. A must in military training, the book survived all these years and has transformed the way we see business today. The lessons that Sun Tzu wrote between battles teach us not only about war, but can also help in the resolution of any modern conflict, including business competition.

Sun Tzu's bases his maxims on his immense knowledge of human nature, and contrary to popular belief, his number one objective was to win without fighting. Modern military training and international policy start from this very principle, and today war is simply a persuasion tool in political negotiations (diplomacy) rather than as the means for achieving the goal. In essence, modern warfare is the last resort in conflict resolution, rather than the preferred method for ensuring our view of the world or desired outcome prevails.

History has taught us that there are no winners when it comes to war. One army may defeat the other, but both have suffered tremendous losses in the process. The failure to find a negotiated way out of the conflict is perhaps both sides' biggest loss. Warfare costs incredible amounts of money, to the detriment of other more important priorities. Economies of smaller countries suffer profound damage during war, and it may take decades to recover from it.

However, when war is inevitable, Sun Tzu takes us through an incredible journey of strategy and tactic development, which focus is to know the enemy well and end the conflict as quickly as possible. Knowing which army has the advantage before the conflict begins is a powerful tactic to determine very early in the process which side will emerge victorious from battle. This has tremendous value in competitive business today.

Learning to assess your enemy's strengths and weaknesses—as well as your own—, and to identify opportunities and threats, is a basic war strategy that has migrated over to the modern business world. Does SWOT analysis sound familiar to you?

How many times have you observed companies naively trying to compete against an invincible competitor, using massive amounts of resources in the attempt? Picking your battles and avoiding unnecessary ones is another wise lesson of general Tzu.

His philosophy was that *"If your forces are ten times superior to those of your adversary, surround them. If they are five times superior, attack them. If they are two times superior, divide them. If your forces are equal in number, fight if possible. However, if your forces are inferior, stay away if you can. And if you are outnumbered, run as fast as you can."*

I do not want this book to become an analysis of Sun Tzu's work. However, I thought it was appropriate and important to include a brief chapter to introduce his millenary teachings and encourage you to pick up a modern version of *The Art of War* and study it, so you can become familiar with how war strategy scenarios apply to the modern business field.

Project managers can learn invaluable lessons from Sun Tzu's teachings, which are useful in finding ways to execute projects that are more successful by avoiding conflict and by having a strategic mind when it comes to dealing with customers and suppliers.

More importantly, by combining this knowledge with the understanding of the PM's role in the business development chain, you can gain access to an elite group of professionals that deliver value to their organizations, not only by executing successful projects, but also by building long-lasting relationships with customers, and by consistently developing new business opportunities.

Know your enemy, avoid conflict, fight if you must, and enjoy the results.

* *The Art of War* is a book originally written by army general Sun Tzu, more than 2,000 years ago and studied, analyzed, and re-edited by several contemporary authors and historians.

Chapter 16

Working with Pyramidal Organizations

The theory of the pyramidal organization is perhaps the best way to illustrate how we all play a role in the revenue-generating process, one way, or another. Similarly, the notion that only certain individuals on the customer side are involved in the vendor selection and purchasing processes is perhaps the worst assumption we can make in the project-based business world.

The truth is that typically many players at different levels in the customer's organization are involved in the buying process; each player thinks differently, acts in a unique way, has personal motivations, is evaluated differently in the organization, and values different aspects of the vendors' offering.

The following simple pyramid diagram can help explain some of the biggest successes and most embarrassing failures in business. If your company is consistently losing orders to one single competitor, time after time, I can almost guarantee that it is due to the fact that this competitor has a thorough understanding of—and is effectively playing at—each of the three levels of the business development pyramid.

Most capital investment projects are conceptualized by a combination of *needs* and/or *desires* from operations people (or end users), business managers, and executives. When trying to select the ideal vendor for the job, all three forces interact with each other, having a definite say in the final decision.

The following diagram illustrates this concept and shows who plays at each level, and what their focus and decision criteria are.

Pyramidal Organization

Operations people are at the base of the pyramid; they are usually concerned with technical aspects of the products and solutions and most of the times make their selections based on price and technical features.

In the middle of the organization, we find management people, who typically deal with business issues and make decisions based on their hot buttons, which usually are Return on Investment (ROI) and Total Cost of Ownership (TCO).

Executives are at the very top of the pyramid, normally preoccupied with the long-term vision of the company, and for that reason make decisions based primarily on value.

The problem is that most salespeople often tackle only one of the three levels of the pyramid, neglecting the other two. There is a natural tendency among salespeople to try to convince the decision-makers in the client organization that their proposal and their products are the best in the market and therefore should be the ones executing the project.

Moreover, it is only natural to have that instinct of bringing the message to the decision-makers, for they are the ones with the ultimate saying when it comes to awarding a project to your company or a competitor. The problem is that the assumption that decision-makers sit at the top of the pyramid is usually wrong.

This *tunnel-vision* approach fails to recognize there are other forces in the client organization that play a significant role in the final award decision. Such is the case of end users, who often have tremendous power when it comes to highlighting the benefits of one product over another, or vetoing one vendor or your own company. Even the most senior executive in the organization typically surrenders to the wishes of the operations group, for they are the ones that have to deal with the product or solution for many years to come and deliver results.

Focusing on the executive level alone is a problem since most executives will often push the decision downward in the organization, instead of putting their neck on the line for choosing the wrong product or vendor, often putting their own integrity in question. At best, when an executive has a clear choice, he or she will find ways to influence their subordinates' minds to pick their favorite candidate, instead of imposing an order vertically.

Every purchase decision has at least three *key players*:

- The executive(s)

- The manager(s)

- The end user(s)

Every group plays a different role and very seldom, a single group has the sole power of making the final decision.

Every purchase decision consists of three *key roles*:

a) Those who actually make the decision.

b) Those with the power to influence the former.

c) And the ones in charge of evaluating the vendors' proposals.

The name of the game is to identify which team members are playing what *role* and tackle them accordingly. What is important here is to realize that all three roles are always in play, even if one player is playing multiple roles. This means we must never neglect any role, and therefore, any player.

The operations people (or level 1) usually focus on technological aspects, product features, reliability, warranty, and service models. Their main concern is usually price and they are very rarely concerned with other elements of the business.

Management plays in the second layer of the pyramid and its attention focuses more on the business side of the procurement process. Their typical language (and hot buttons) revolves around concepts such as *Return on Investment* and *Total Cost of Ownership*. They usually have Profit and Loss responsibility in the organization, so they are not as concerned with operational aspects of the resulting decision, but mostly with overall financial results. In other words, the investment decision must make financial sense for them, and the selected vendor must be able to guarantee a successful implementation, which they measure based on previous experience in similar jobs.

At the top of the pyramid (level 3) we find the executives, who are rarely concerned with technical aspects or preoccupied with routine business issues. Instead, their minds are concentrated on value. Executives are in nature forward thinkers and their motivations are not in the present, but in the future. Their primary focus is to accomplish a vision.

Several years ago, I asked Dave Jardine—who wrote the prologue of this book—why I did not see much of him anymore. His answer was *"I'm sitting in my office George, thinking, and envisioning the future."* His words carried significant weight with me over the years, and took on a completely new dimension when I started to study decision-making and leadership models.

For executives, every penny spent must bring something of value to the organization. The product will perform its basic function as promised, that is a given; if not somebody will be fired. The project will be financially sound; if not someone will be fired.

Following are some of the key questions we must ask ourselves when dealing at the C-level:

1. Will the project help fulfill the company's vision?

2. Will it bring real value to the organization?

3. Will it help differentiate your customer's company from their own competitors?

4. Will the result of implementing this project have a positive impact on shareholders' value?

5. Will it improve your client's own professional reputation before his or her board of directors?

Most salespeople play at one level of this pyramid. Good salespeople can play in two levels. Very few business development experts are capable of dealing in all three levels. The important message here to remember is that the three levels exist, and that the best strategy to securing more orders for your company is to model a plan to tackle all three levels of this pyramid using the resources at your disposal.

As a project manager, you are most likely dealing in level 1, since your project counterparts are probably in that area of the pyramid as well. Occasionally you may be asked to join meetings with level 2 members, but rarely will you interact with someone in level 3.

A team approach is required to have permanent presence in all three levels of the pyramid. Sales teams usually take care of level 2, while VPs and CEOs play in level 3. You are the best resource to keep your level 1 counterpart happy, solving their problems, and building and delivering successful projects. Nevertheless, do not be surprised if your visits to level 2 management become more frequent as your projects become more successful.

We talked about *Time & Event* strategy and the importance of placing the right resources in front of the customer at the right time. The most successful business development strategy is the one that works without the need of sales tactics.

Let me illustrate:

One of the companies I consulted for had a project manager and a subject matter expert so well entrenched in the customer's organization that they were able to bring new orders consistently over a period of about 10 years without a single salesperson ever visiting the client. What a concept!

The person(s) communicating with the customer should always deliver a cohesive message, no matter who is delivering it, and no matter who the recipient is. More importantly, whatever promises are made in one level must be achievable by the rest of the organization.

A typical mistake we observe in pyramid selling is that your CEO makes promises at Level 3 committing your team to delivering impossible results, putting immense amounts of pressure on your manager and yourself. In the end, this translates into project failure and customer frustration, which, as we learned, signifies loss of revenue, sales decline, profit erosion, etc.

Chapter 17

Project Pricing Models

Project managers always face the challenging task of delivering a project that not only is on schedule and delivers positive results to the customer, but that is also profitable for their company. Doing so successfully is a PM's core competency, so management's expectation is that they will have no problems delivering a financially successful project.

The problem comes when the project has insufficient funds or an unrealistic schedule, facts that seriously hinder your chances of ensuring a successful execution. This is what we call an *undersold project*. What should a PM do when faced with such a project? —The very first thing you should do when receiving an undersold project is to perform a thorough analysis of the resources (human, material, and financial) you will need to guarantee a successful execution, add the necessary funds, people, and time to the original budget, and get your management to agree to the new plan.

I call this action re-planning, re-scheduling, and re-budgeting a project. The strategy may also include the preparation of a comprehensive schedule and margin recovery plan, aimed at doing everything possible to return the project to a *healthier* state.

Once management approves the newly defined project objectives, you must commit to the new results, and work diligently to deliver a successful project under the new terms. Typically, companies evaluate project managers' performance based on their ability to deliver successful projects, the way the company defines success, ignoring what a successful project means to customers.

An undersold project is a perfect recipe for failure, so why would you ever consider committing yourself to successfully completing an underfunded project? You must re-define the project and expectations first and then work hard to deliver on those new (more realistic) parameters. If your recovery plans work, then you will be able to deliver even better results, which would come as a bonus.

Who is to blame?

Let us dig deeper on this issue for a moment. Why would your sales team undersell a project in the first place? Why would management authorize to sign a contract for a project with such conditions? The answer lies in the principles of *pricing* and *price competition.*

In the project world, vendors usually calculate the price that a customer receives as part of a proposal as a function of the estimation of the following elements:

- Cost (products, parts, labor, subcontractors, travel & living, etc.); plus
- SG&A (Sales, General, and Administration expenses); plus
- Risk Factors; plus
- Profit (or Margin)

The project-based industry typically accepts this pricing model practice, so we automatically assume there is nothing wrong with it. However, after careful examination we can conclude there are a few fundamental problems that progressively appear with this cost-plus-margin *vicious cycle.*

Yes, a never-ending spiral problem that worsens with every project execution and with every new tender process. Have you ever witnessed a project that fails to deliver profits to the organization? What typically happens when a project goes wrong?

Projects may get in the red for a variety of reasons and though the analysis of those reasons shall not be topic of discussion in the pages of this book, I feel it is important to analyze the impact that an unsuccessful project may have in the long-term business success of the corporation as a whole.

When a project incurs a loss, the corporation incurs a loss; and when many projects are not delivering profitable results, we are facing a chronic problem that is slowly eroding the complete viability of the corporation. For-profit companies, including project-based organizations, must maintain an ongoing concern in order to continue to exist, and when project profits start to decline, we must react quickly to identify the main issues that are causing this margin erosion.

Once we have clearly identified the sources of the problem, the next step is to take corrective action aimed at solving the problems at the base, so profitability can promptly return and the company can continue its course.

Unfortunately, more often than not we observe that company leaders are quick to blame the sales process for such losses, failing to implement a 360-degree analysis of the problem. I am not suggesting that the sales function is always perfect and that mistakes never occur in that group. Estimation and pricing errors are always possible, but we should never consider them the sole cause of the problem.

What is concerning here is the spiral effect that project execution problems have in the bid preparation cycles. Inevitably, it is our nature to want to avoid making the same mistake twice, and the next time we face the opportunity to prepare a proposal for another project, past failures can significantly affect our confidence level in our own estimations, which reflects on future bids.

Corporations impose tremendous pressure not only on project execution teams, but also on the sales group to insure the next project stays on track and delivers positive results. What is our answer ninety percent of the time? —We introduce a correction multiplier to the execution estimations on top of risk factors, resulting on a higher project cost, which according to the traditional pricing model described above, in the end produces a higher price for the customer.

The real question here is: What do we do when the next project also fails to deliver profitable results? —You guessed it, we again conclude that our estimation skills need revision and we quickly introduce corrections to our effort estimations, and so the cycle repeats itself.

The real problem with this spiral model is that soon enough our company will start losing orders, for customers do not have ever-growing budgets to keep pace with our ever-increasing prices. The moment our company starts losing orders we start observing the real implications of this pricing model, which slowly but surely jeopardizes the ongoing concern of the corporation.

Once you and your colleagues start to question how your competition is able to secure project after project at significantly lower prices, it is time to introduce change, and fast. This is the moment we all realize that something is wrong.

Perhaps the easiest way to understand how distant this pricing exercise is from other models is by analyzing how prices work in the consumer goods and services industry.

A different approach

Have you ever stopped to question how the prices of items such as shoes, watches, shirts, mobile phones, even a cup of coffee are determined? Can you explain why a pair of shoes can sell for prices that go from the thrifty to the exclusive luxury level?

Think about it, a simple item which basic function is to cover and protect our feet while walking can successfully sell for less than $50, more than $100, $500, $1,500, even $5,000 dollars or more!

How is this possible? —The explanation can be found in one of the most fundamental elements of economics and consumer product pricing: The *willingness to pay* concept. In willingness to pay-based pricing, marketing experts evaluate the *maximum* amount of money that a *target group* is *willing* to pay for the *perceived* benefits (value) of a certain product or service.

In other words, a company designed a product or service with a clear target audience in mind, considering socio-economic status and other demographic elements. Once experts select the targeted demographic group and conceive the product or service, they study how much money that consumer group is *willing* to pay to acquire the good or service in the marketplace.

A key element when determining willingness to pay is the *perceived* benefits the consumer will receive in return for his or her money. In different terms, what value the consumer receives by purchasing a certain product or service, at a certain price.

As we discussed in an earlier chapter, the perceived value of the products and services we consume are highly influenced by marketing and advertising campaigns, designed to position them at the right level (alignment) with the targeted demographic group. Through carefully designed marketing and advertising strategies, companies can highlight the attributes (real and otherwise) of their products and services; and sometimes even assign certain characteristics that products do not even possess.

This way, a pair of high-heel shoes can be presented as a luxurious accessory that enhances the look of females of a certain demographic group, characterized by successful and independent women that dress elegantly and always look good, that drive a certain type of vehicle, and that like to frequent a certain type of restaurant, bar, or night club.

A thirty-second TV commercial can be very effective when it comes to positioning a product like this. Through the study of income levels of the different socio-economic groups, marketing experts can easily determine the maximum price an AB female, for example, is *willing* to pay for such a pair of high-heel shoes. The more status the image of the product is able to transmit, the higher the price certain groups of consumers are willing to pay. As discussed in a previous chapter, high-heel shoes can easily be transformed into bottles of water in the desert, so to speak.

With that number as a starting point, consumer product companies perform what can only be described as a **Reverse Price-Engineering** exercise to find the most cost-effective way of producing the product with the promised features and qualities, so acceptable profits can be realized. They are constantly reviewing and revising their production models, in order to maximize profitability in the long run. This explains the commonly observed off shoring of the manufacturing process, for example.

Steve Jobs was famous for dictating the sell price of the products (and services) he envisioned long before the company designed them or put them into production. He had an intimate knowledge of the audience he wanted to target; and more importantly, he knew exactly how to infuse a product with a special aura (marketing) that would allow his company to demand high prices from a very broad target audience (willingness to pay).

What high-heel shoes, Apple products, and projects have in common? —Not much really, but the lessons we can learn from the willingness to pay-based pricing model can be successfully transferred to the traditional costing-base project pricing.

Let us go back to our swimming pool construction project example for a minute. Assume the pool company had failed to deliver profitable projects for the last two years, and their only solution to the problem has been a continuous contingency cost increase, with its subsequent (and damaging) customer price increases.

Would you have selected an obviously overpriced proposal? — Most likely not. Does this mean that pool construction companies never face unsuccessful projects? —Of course not. The answer lies in the willingness to pay principle and in the *reverse price-engineering* practice.

When a project fails to deliver profitable results, we must honestly analyze our execution model. Do we have the correct resources? Are we as project managers unnecessarily over-spending? Are we taking advantage of all possible synergies in the project and the organization, avoiding as much as possible *re-inventing the wheel* every time? Are we truly challenging our execution process, constantly looking for ways to optimize results, or are we simply following the establishment, falling victims of the status quo? Are we really driving the customers, engaging and energizing them to do their part in helping us maintain schedule?

Injecting an extra quota of conservationism and contingency to our costing sheets will inevitably increase our prices, seriously hurting our company's viability in the long run. This practice will—eventually—put our business unit, division, or entire company out of business.

Our calculation sheets should not be the only basis for a project price. Instead, the market should define prices based on the market's willingness to pay for the type of project the customer is interested in building. Project-based companies must then perform *reverse price engineering* to find the most effective way of executing the project for the maximum price the target market is willing to pay. If the project cost structure allows it, companies can adjust the price in order to increase the chances of winning the project.

This implies we have to take a very serious look at our marketing practices, for an intimate knowledge of our customer and the marketplace is essential to a successful implementation of this model. At the same time, our branding strategies must be in optimal alignment with the desired results, so *value selling* can be facilitated.

This last aspect is essential to prevent margin-erosion or unsuccessful projects. When the branding efforts are not properly aligned with our pricing strategy, our sales team will not be able to successfully perform *value selling*. In other words, we will not be able to demand the *maximum* amount of money the market is *willing* to pay our team to build and deliver the project.

Companies are always looking for ways to differentiate themselves from the competition, so they can perform as close as possible to the maximum willingness to pay level. A successfully executed marketing and branding strategy, coupled with the right pricing model, should allow any vendor to differentiate its company, products, and services clearly from the competition, and to demand the maximum price for them. This is the key to profitability, together with an optimized project execution model.

Price should never be the issue...

Customers are always willing to pay a premium for a differentiated product, service, or project. Differentiating factors must be clear and demonstrable, and must offer significant value to the customer (see the Pyramidal Organizations chapter), so that they are willing to pay more for something unique, or that at least *appears* to be unique.

Price should never be the center of discussion with our customers, period. If your company's salespeople or you engage in price arguments with a customer, chances are your projects will not be successful. If your company is forced into making pricing concessions, as a way to secure contracts, then obviously there is something wrong with your organization's marketing and branding strategies, for clear differentiation was not possible.

Michael Vickers says it beautifully in his book: *"Price should never be the issue, unless it is the issue, and when price is the issue, it is the only issue..."*

When our prices are the highest in the marketplace, far surpassing what customers are willing to pay, it becomes increasingly more difficult for salespeople to convince customers that our projects, products, and services are better, more efficient, faster, less contaminant, or with higher ROI than those of the competition.

If the value that our products, services, and projects offer to the marketplace is low, willingness to pay will always be low, and therefore we will never be able to demand high prices from our customers. If, on the other hand, we find ways to increase the value our products, services, and projects have to offer, then we have the customers' attention, so long as we understand value the way they do.

This is fundamentally the reason why costing-base pricing continues to fail at project-based corporations and companies continue to struggle for survival. The answer to break free from this company-sinking trap is a humble and sincere analysis of our product development and project execution practices, together with a professionally designed reverse price-engineering model, based on the market's willingness to pay for what we offer.

If a simple commodity device invented to protect our feet while we walk can sell for as little as $20 and for as much as $5,000 dollars or more, then our products and projects can too.

If we find it difficult to demand the prices we want for our goods and services, because the market is not willing to pay as much, the problem is not with the customers, the market, or with our competitors. The root of the problem is in how the marketplace perceives the value of our goods and services. The only solution to the problem is to change that perception.

A good place to start is with people; how much value are our teams bringing to the table? What can we do to improve that perception of value? Do we understand value the way our customers do? Is our company enabling us to maximize the value we offer our customers, the way they define it?

So, next time you are looking at a pair of shoes or a new watch, ask yourself *"How much am I willing to pay for this item? How much value do I put on owning it?"* It is interesting to perform this simple exercise during holidays such as Valentines, for example. On February 14th of each year, men are *willing* to pay almost anything for a bouquet of roses! (The price we would have to pay for coming home empty-handed is simply too high to bear).

On this particular day, we give a commodity item such as flowers the highest value they will ever have and we are willing to pull our credit cards and pay almost anything for a nice bouquet. Now, if you are already late coming home, forget *nice*, <u>any</u> bouquet will do. At that point, we do not even ask for the price anymore. All of a sudden, a dozen of roses became a bottle of water in the middle of the desert.

Chapter 18

PMs and Social Networks

Everything we do in our personal and professional lives involves interaction with others. As a project manager, you have a team of talented individuals that need direction, coaching, and motivation. You also interact with colleagues from other departments within your own organization, like legal, human resources, sales, R&D, etc.

Outside the boundaries of your company, your role offers multiple situations whereby you need to engage in permanent dialog not only with your customers, but also with other parties, such as subcontractors, suppliers, consultants, regulators, etc.

Over the years, we build an ever-growing network of contacts and often we underestimate the real power of those who belong to the group of individuals that at some point we had the privilege of meeting.

Perhaps now is a good time to revisit the chapter on Leverage, since there is a close link between what we are discussing here and what we covered in those pages.

For your network of contacts to be effective, you must invest time and effort in it. In other words, simply wrapping a collection of business cards with an elastic band is certainly not a good example of building an effective network of contacts. Having hundreds of contacts in your LinkedIn[®], Twitter[®], or Facebook[®] accounts does not necessarily mean you have an effective social network either.

I asked you to revisit the chapter on Leverage because the main reason for anybody to build a network of contacts is to be able to use it later. This also means that we, as members of this social network, are also willing to serve those that invest in fostering a fruitful relationship with us. This is what I define as the reciprocating behavior, which is essential to building a fair and effective social network.

The key ingredient to having an effective network of contacts is to invest seriously in the personal relationships that are at the very foundation of the social groups to which we belong. Relationship-based leverage is all about giving, doing, and lending a helpful hand to others when they need it most. This may mean simple things, like passing on a piece of news you found on the web that could be useful to one of your contacts, inviting someone to lunch or coffee, being available for a referral call, lending this or any other book to a friend, etc.

Having a collection of contacts will not give you leverage, ever. Investing in the personal relationships with those in your social network will definitively pay off. Get to know your contacts, spend time with them, and allow them to get to know you better; understand their motivations and challenges, offer to help whenever possible, and accept their help when offered to you. Only then, will you have an effective social network, a true resource to your personal and business growth.

Therefore, the next time you ask a friend or an acquaintance for a job referral or to babysit your kids, ask yourself if you have done enough for them in the first place. You cannot all of a sudden ask someone you have not been in touch with for more than 30 years if you can stay at their house while visiting their country. That not only is inappropriate, but it also contradicts all the rules of proper network building. The right thing to do is to invest in those relationships permanently, so then you can ask for such a favor when the time comes.

Project management networking

The importance of effective social networking transcends those in sales or business development roles. Project managers, service, and technical professionals should also understand the power of building and nurturing an effective network. Do it with fellow PMs, engineers, and professionals in all disciplines. Take advantage of networking events, such as trade shows and conferences. Get out of the shell, meet people far beyond the reach of your profession or career, and develop strong relationships that you will be able to carry with you for decades to come.

The same applies to your newly assigned project. The very first thing a PM should do when accepting a new project is go and meet his or her customer face to face, regardless of geographic location. No matter how expensive it might seem; investing in building a personal relationship with your counterpart as soon as possible will bring dividends that far exceed the cost of that trip.

Meeting your customers face to face is not enough though. Make sure you get to know them personally and ensure they get to know you as well. Open up first, so they can reciprocate. Pay attention to little details, like objects in your customer's office, for example. Does he have a golf trophy on the table or an autographed baseball? Perhaps there is a miniature F-1 car model, or a picture of his family? Those little details give us clues as to what interests the individual may have. Use them as an excuse to inquire about what you see, and if you share similar interests show how passionate you are about them.

We all have some things in common with most people; we just have to learn to identify the aspects that make us connect. A Professional Engineer denomination, for example, sometimes is enough to spark a more personal conversation. Things like vacation trips, food, wine, sports, schools, children, cars, motorcycles, or gadgets of various types are the most common topics used to break the ice and connect at a more personal—sometimes banal—level during a first meeting. Only one piece of advice: Avoid discussing politics and religion at all costs. Those are not appropriate topics for a first meeting discussion.

Trying to find something in common with your client is one of the easiest ways to start building a personal relationship. Tell them your story, listen to their stories with attention, and find ways to connect. After you return from your trip, follow up, not only on project related matters, but also at a personal level:

- *"Dear Mark, I know how passionate you are about F-1, I thought you would enjoy this picture I took next to Jacques Villeneuve at his Newtown Bar & Restaurant in Montreal a few years ago during race week. I hope you like it. Best regards."*

(As an aside note, it is interesting to observe that "Newtown" is the English translation of Jacques' French last name, which in itself is a great branding move).

I know it sounds trivial, but little details like this will help you break the ice that typically surrounds business relationships, allowing you to build a warmer, long-lasting friendship. Never confuse friendship with a less demanding customer though. You may very well become friends, but that does not mean your clients now have to be more lenient and more forgiving towards the quality of the work you and your team do for them. Be very clear on this and make sure they know you are clear on it as well. They will appreciate it and you will earn their respect.

Last week I met a new client and during the meeting he noticed my USB pen drive with a logo of my favorite car brand, which happened to be his favorite car brand as well. He loved the item so much that as soon as I returned home I picked up a new pen drive at my car dealership and sent it to him as a token of appreciation for receiving me and spending time with me. He wrote me a friendly thank you note. We may never do business together, but now I have a new friend in my network.

If you meet someone on a flight, by all means, engage in conversation and exchange contact details, and make sure you follow up with a note or an invitation to join your LinkedIn page:

> - *"Dear Lindsey, it was great meeting you on the flight to Dallas last week. I hope you had a successful stay in the city and an uneventful return home. I remember you mentioned you were planning a vacation trip to Peru in a couple of months with your husband. Please find attached a list of restaurants I definitively recommend in Lima. You are going to love the food there. Best regards."*

You never know when you are going to need the help of someone. Make sure you have invested in building a strong personal relationship with those in your social network, so you can ask for help when needed.

Chapter 19

The Color of a Successful Project

As I indicated at the beginning, this book does not intent to transform project managers, service, and technical team members into salespeople, nor does it pretend to teach you how to run projects successfully. I suspect you have taken significant training and read enough books on this topic already. I thought, however, that I could briefly share some ideas here to complement the subject of this book, and in doing so help you see the color of a successful project in a different light.

We have analyzed the importance of marketing and branding, of building effective social networks, and of utilizing all types of leveraging. We have also reviewed different kinds of strategies, from the teachings of Sun Tzu to the game of chess. We also studied pricing models and learned how customers buy. When analyzing value selling and customer satisfaction we concluded that happy customers are the key to repeat-business and more new customers.

The project teams' ability to run successful projects (the way the customer defines success) is perhaps the most valuable tool CEOs have today to ensure the sustainability of the company in the long run. We have already established that no matter how many new salespeople we bring into the organization, we will continue to lose orders and customers; and consequently revenue and profits will inevitably suffer, unless we consistently impress our customers with outstanding projects and service.

My message to any boardroom executive would be that hiring and training the sales force is very important, but that alone will not create the necessary change to drive revenue figures in the right direction. They have to start spending more resources in training project managers and delivery teams, not only on their own competencies, but also on anything that helps them understand and embrace their role in the business development efforts of the corporation.

Some may argue that training people is a moot point, because of the risk of them leaving the company and taking the new knowledge with them elsewhere. I think the real problem occurs when we do not provide our people with enough good training opportunities and they end up staying instead.

Executing a successful project for both your customer and your employer is a delicate balancing act that requires the project manager and every team member to wear two hats at all times. This seems to be a good analogy for the traditional way of evaluating projects. However, we are here to challenge the established paradigms and to promote a new way of helping our companies thrive, and not to simply re-write the book on the accepted norm.

I have seen project-based companies achieve tremendous growth by focusing on the customer first, no matter the costs. I have also seen my share of companies undo their own success by shifting their model to a more bottom-line oriented approach. A model that puts incredible amounts of attention to corporate immobilizing rules that compensate individuals for the defense of the profit line at all costs and penalize the construction of a successful project the way the customer defines and measures it.

The price that corporations have to pay for always putting the customer first no matter what, can easily be recovered in the long run by capitalizing on the positive reviews, repeat-business opportunities, increased market share, competitor isolation, and advocacy gained as a result. All these factors together contribute to an increased value of the company as a whole, regardless of whether it is a private or a public corporation.

On the other hand, when project-based companies put the bottom line first, the complete corporate culture suffers, shifting the attention to the balance sheet, rather than to the person that signs the contracts and approves our invoices in the first place.

We can observe behavioral changes everywhere in the organization, from the receptionist that answers the phone and greets visitors, to the VPs and CEOs that deliver branding messages on a daily basis. Clients notice this behavior quickly, who grow disappointed and frustrated with projects that move too slow and do not meet their expectations, and people that simply do not seem to care about them or the success of their projects.

Imagine for a moment that your cable or satellite provider did not care about you (the customer) anymore and their focus shifted elsewhere instead. If your receiver broke, they will not be prompt to replace it, and when they do, they will charge you for it. If half your channels disappeared, bringing them back will not be a priority. If your problem required a technician to visit you in the house, you will receive a bill for his time.

If you felt you were paying too much for the service, they will simply let you go to the competition, rather than doing the impossible to keep you as a satisfied, paying customer. Giving you a month's service free of charge or lowering your monthly bill is not even an option, for those measures would negatively affect the bottom line. In this environment, such actions are not even possible.

If you are building a technologically intense project that included 4 days of training for the customer, who later asks you for the possibility of taking an extra day of training before returning home, and you answer with a change order quote, most likely you work for a bottom line-driven company, rather than for a customer-centric organization.

Nevertheless, building a customer-centric company is no trivial task. Corporations cannot achieve this goal without the help of every employee, particularly those who spend most of their time facing the client (you). Project managers and technical people interacting with customers have the responsibility of making the client feel important, cared for, and looked after. Project teams not only build the projects the company is contractually obligated to deliver, but they also assist customers with daily issues, helping them resolve the problems that keep them awake at night.

The *wow* factor

I have learned a great deal about customer satisfaction by simply reading restaurant consumer reviews. Time after time consumers do not give businesses the maximum score of five stars because they failed to deliver either a *wow* food experience, or a *wow* customer experience.

It is a revelation to read reviews that praise a restaurant for its amazing food, but wish the waiters were more attentive and professional, or that they did not have to wait so long for a table or for the food to arrive. There is always a little something that makes the consumer remove points and deliver the always destructive *"loved the food, but will not be going back due to the poor service"* type of phrase.

On the other hand, it is common to find reviews that praise the customer experience, but put the menu on a more forgiving light. Astonishingly, comments like *"food was average, but the atmosphere, decor, and customer service were amazing. I'm definitively going back to this place"* are not rare, and for this reason restaurant owners are shifting their strategies to focus more on the complete customer experience side of the equation, rather than on the food itself.

In our case, the equation is a bit more complex than that. The food (the projects we execute) is as important as the customer experience. Project-based companies need to find the right balance between delivering a successful project, both for the customer and the corporation, all the while wowing the customer with quality service and outstanding project management.

Finding the sweet spot on that invisible sliding bar that selects how much attention we put to the bottom line and corporate rules, versus how much we care for the customer, is the key to a successful project-driven organization. Companies cannot survive without either of the two and will definitively disappear (or at least suffer tremendous losses) if we move the sliding bar too close to either extreme, regardless of which one.

Customer   S u c c e s s Z o n e   Corporation

The role of the project manager consequently is to help the company find that perfect balance and to make every effort to ensure the whole team is concerned with wowing the customer every day. Even if the corporate rules dictate that we should only care about cost and profitability, it is the PM's responsibility to deliver three basic things at the end of the day:

1. A successful project completed on time and without deficiencies,
2. A satisfied customer willing to return and to advocate; and
3. A profitable result for the corporation

Corporate erosion

If we are not able to achieve any of these three fundamental objectives, we are putting the viability of the complete company at risk. I call this *Corporate Erosion*, which is a slow occurring phenomenon that affects the performance of project-based companies over time. Multiple factors can affect financial results, including some that are completely outside our control, but they are also—and most definitively—affected by project performance.

If a project fails to deliver a profitable result it will ultimately have a negative impact on the corporate financial results. If it is an isolated case, the success of other projects can easily compensate the losses. However, if project margin erosion is a chronic problem, then the impact that those poor project results have on the corporate balance sheet becomes paramount, and if no corrective action is taken promptly, the viability and very existence of the company will be at risk.

We already studied how corporations are quick to implement measures to contain and prevent project margin loss. However, the problem is that those measures typically involve loading future project proposals with unnecessary risk funds and pessimistic estimations that result in non-competitive pricing, which—far from fixing the problem—put the company's viability at even greater risk by losing too many orders consecutively, damaging the company's brand.

If we deliver a very profitable project with a very unhappy customer, we are not making much progress either. Though the corporate balance sheet will look great and the PM and execution team will get their bonuses, *corporate erosion* continues to occur, almost invisibly. Customers that feel dissatisfied will never come back for more, and what is worse; they will never recommend our products, our people, and our company to others. The result is an inexplicable process that slowly (and literally) shrinks the size of our business, year after year.

How does the corporation react to these results? –They fire the CEO, or the VP of sales, and even some sales staff. They bring in new executives and more sales professionals, for that is the only way to recover the market share previous executives managed to give away to the competition.

The new team decides it is time to attack competitors aggressively by lowering prices of new proposals. When we start to see some project wins, we think the lower pricing strategy is working and it is time to celebrate. Nevertheless, when those projects are complete a few months (or years) later, we observe even greater margin erosion, often resulting in significant losses that have an even deeper impact on the balance sheet.

It seems that no matter what project-based companies do to fix the problem; the results are always the same: Decreasing sales, loss of market share, profit erosion, and overruns. A chaotic environment that prompts difficult decisions; complete teams are let go and it is not rare to see hurting companies be acquired at bargain prices by healthier competitors.

Why so many organizations fail to see the obvious? Perhaps the answer lies in one of the most basic corporate practices: Incentives. The human species—like most animals—easily respond to stimulus. We raise our children utilizing different forms of incentives to obtain desired behaviors or results. We train our domestic pets in a similar way; once we observe the desired behavior, the animal receives a prize in return; it is a win-win situation.

Corporate incentive packages are simply the means for rewarding desired results. For-profit organizations seem to be obsessed with growth; and typically do not reward behaviors that do not directly contribute to the corporation's quest for growth.

Why it is that companies regard not growing as a failure? What is wrong with having a successful business that delivers outstanding customer results and profitable projects, but that does not grow? Is there something wrong with a steady performance? Who invented this model? —I have had several heated discussions on this subject with executives and MBA professors over the years. We have not been able to reach a clear conclusion, but had agreed that perhaps it is more of a philosophical topic, rather than technical.

Harvesting

We tend to have a drastic, very direct way of dealing with issues in our lives. If it rains, we open an umbrella –problem solved. If it is too hot, we turn the air conditioner on –problem solved. If we have a headache, we take a pill. If we need more money, we work overtime or find a second job. If we are hungry, we eat. If we are not happy with our spouse, we get divorced.

We like quick results, we are not patient, and we do not like to deal with the root of the problems that affect our daily lives. If a tooth aches, we take a pill or get the cavity filled. If we want entertainment, we watch TV.

We do not investigate why we have headaches, or why our teeth are decaying, or why we (feel that) need more money, or why we are not happy in our relationships. Instead of taking corrective measures at the source of the problems, we simply get rid of them as quickly as possible.

If we have weeds infesting our lawn, we spray it with weed-killing chemicals, instead of getting on our knees and digging a hole to remove the weeds from the roots.

Something similar occurs in corporations today. Since the ultimate goal is growth (by increasing revenues and margins) then the only way to achieve that objective is to increase sales and profits, year after year. What is the obvious strategy? –We hire more sales staff and we offer incentives for people to pay special attention to cost-cutting measures and anything that promotes helping profitability every quarter and by the end of the fiscal year.

Obviously investing in creating a happy customer that may or may not return with another project in three or five years does not seem aligned with the short-term view of increasing profitability by the end of each quarter or fiscal year. Therefore, companies do not reward this behavior. Corporations by definition compensate short-term results, especially publicly traded ones.

This explains why publicly traded companies must announce financial performance results on a quarterly basis. This is the extreme of short-term vision, for nothing can change in such a short time. The main objective of public companies is to increase the stock price, and a bad quarter result would only have the opposite effect. This creates an environment whereby companies only reward those behaviors that directly contribute to improving next quarter's financial results.

This affects not only C-level executives, but project managers as well, and virtually every employee in the corporation. Nobody has the mandate (and therefore the incentive) to build the financial results of three years down the road. Only the current fiscal year is of importance and everything else is secondary. The problem is that the very same measures we take today to ensure a successful fiscal year are the ones destroying—or at least hurting—our results three years later.

Put in perspective, if corporations rewarded forward think-ing and those who invest time and effort in building the future of the company, we would observe how the future quickly becomes the present, and then by continuing to invest in the future, we would continue to create a brighter present. It is like seeding and taking care of the crop; if done correctly we will have a harvest every year. However, if seeding, watering, fertilizing, and every other daily activity necessary to care for the crop is done wrong, a successful harvest will not be possible.

Farmers can teach us a very valuable lesson here, for they are never concerned with harvesting every quarter. They understand the importance of time and daily work to ensure a fruitful result in due time. More importantly, they are patient; they know that if they do everything right and if normal weather conditions exist, they will always have successful harvesting.

If companies were run with more patience and with a satisfied customer in mind at all times, executives would reward behaviors that seek sound financial results not only this or next quarter, but also in the next year, and the year after that.

Project managers should be as concerned with delivering a profitable project for their employers, as with investing in delivering a successful project for their customer. These elements are the pillars to the future of your company.

Professional project managers should never compromise on this, since their own reputation is on the line as well. In today's digital world it is not rare to find PMs and customers connecting in professional networks such as LinkedIn. Nothing will hurt your own career more than a customer not willing to endorse your skills and to provide a good reference for your next job.

I am the biggest enemy of any extremes and I am convinced that the secret to success lies on an optimal balance between customer focus and short-term financial results. It is a difficult equation to solve, for the absence of one prevents the existence of the other. Without customers, there will be no bottom line, and without a financially sound company, it would be very difficult to obtain and keep customers.

I understand why the corporate world works the way it does today, but I am also suggesting we spend time experimenting with new formulas, shifting the invisible sliding bar ever so slightly in the opposite direction and see what happens.

Chapter 20

Business Pouring Down the Funnel

I have already written a fair deal about reward systems, and perhaps I have criticized somewhat the way corporations are rewarding what I believe to be the wrong behaviors today, at least short-term behaviors. We have also analyzed the destructive effects of short-term vision and how the demand for immediate results is hindering the company's ability to thrive in the long run.

We already established that we respond to stimulus and will usually develop behaviors and performance patterns that respond to motivating agents, like bonuses, extra vacation days, recognition, promotions, or anything that we consider valuable.

It all seems to make sense, but as we discovered in the preceding chapter, sometimes corporations are incentivizing the wrong behaviors. It appears to be logical to reward actions to secure this year's orders and protect the profit line. However, what are the long-term effects of today's actions?

Being concerned with short-term results is not necessarily wrong and I completely understand why companies must focus their efforts in the current year's top and bottom lines. The key is to allow space for visionaries and to reward those that work to protect tomorrow's balance sheet as well. Such is the case of progressive marketing groups, for example.

A few years ago, I met a business leader who runs a very successful company with a unique sales model. He has two very distinct sales groups. He calls the first *Short-Term Sales* and the other *Long-Term Sales*. As you are probably guessing, the first group has short-term targets with the appropriate incentives, while the latter has long-term goals with the corresponding reward system.

The Short-Term Sales team is banned from investing any effort whatsoever in pursuing mid to long-term business opportunities. Furthermore, they do not receive rewards for any type of long-term behavior. Their only mandate is to reach for the *low hanging fruit* and secure immediate projects for the corporation.

The Long-Term Sales team, by contrast, cannot spend any time in pursuing or closing immediate business opportunities. Their compensation plan is 100% aligned with long-term results only. Their only job is to protect the brand and company's reputation, paving the road for future business success. Their phone calls are not to try to secure the next order, but to discuss customers' investment strategies, to invite them to the next industry trade show or corporate golf tournament, or to resolve any quality and service issues.

Their job is to ensure customers have an incredible experience every time they interact with the company and to guarantee every phone call is returned promptly, every request for support is followed through, and every problem is quickly resolved beyond expectations.

They design and implement technical seminars and road shows, perform customer feedback sessions to guide their product R&D investments, and make sure the company understands how the customers' industry is evolving, so they can adapt with it.

When I visited my friend's company for the first time I immediately noticed a special attention to detail, as the receptionist greeted me by my last name before I even introduced myself.

When I asked my friend about his marketing department, he shockingly said, *"I do not need one; my long-term sales group already achieves the true objectives of a marketing department."* I thought about it for a while and concluded that if what we need is some brochures, a logo, a colorful website, and a handful of trade shows a year, then we do not need a full marketing department. What his LTS group was doing was delivering <u>true marketing value</u>.

His reinvented marketing team was delivering real and measureable results: A strong brand clearly aligned and recognized in the marketplace, a clear marketing campaign, and outstanding customer experiences every time. More importantly, the LTS group was also actively engaging potential clients (new and repeat), pursuing projects that were set out to start at least three to five years down the road.

It is very similar to what occurs during *American Idol*. While we watch the show live on TV, the production team is working tirelessly to have everything ready for the auditions for next season. The show ends in May and audition tours for the next season begin in July; and while auditions take place and are recorded throughout the summer months, there is another production team preparing for what will be the airing of the next season in the spring.

It is truly a relay race, where hundreds of professionals work very hard to find the contestants for the upcoming season, record every audition, edit the material, and get it ready for broadcasting, while the other team gets ready to take that input and produce the show we watch on TV. The collaboration and dedication of the two teams is what makes the show a success year after year.

People in the Long Term Sales group are forward thinkers; their minds are in tomorrow. They are not concerned with the company's next quarter results, not even with the current fiscal year's balance sheet. Their compensation packages only reward long-term behavior and a strong commitment with customer success and the sustainability of the business.

My friend explained to me that after only a few years, he never had to worry about short-term results anymore. His redefined *marketing* team had done such a good job that all he needed was a select group of sales professionals to secure (close) the projects that were literally pouring down the funnel.

Thanks to the job done by the long-term sales team, closing the current year's business opportunities was a very smooth process. Customers wanted to do business with this company and its people; they did not want any other vendor touching their projects. Their brand recognition and reputation were such, that all they had to do is ensure they had the best resources building successful projects for their customers and investing in protecting the present and securing the future.

From the moment I first visited to my friend's company a few years back, I understood the real importance of delivering outstanding customer experiences and investing as much as possible in future fiscal years, as in immediate results. I learned more about repeat business and advocacy in a one day visit to his company than I did in many years of professional career and even MBA classroom time.

Let us go back now to our swimming pool construction project once again. You may think that in this case investing in customer satisfaction is not as important as in other situations. After all, who needs to build a swimming pool more than once in a lifetime? You may be surprised to learn how many people sell their homes and want to build a new pool in their next house. In addition, word of mouth remains today the most effective form of advertising and the possibilities are endless when it comes to selling by referral.

Those contractors that *nickel & dime* the client for every single little detail that is not part of the contract are usually the ones that customers will not remember. More importantly, those that play games with customers or that use unethical tricks to increase the booked value of the jobs by inconspicuously excluding aspects that are expectedly part of the basic project delivery, are usually short-term players. Referral business is obviously non-existent for these types of vendors.

However, some project-based companies not only end up tricking themselves out of business, but also manage to disappoint their customers deeply during project execution. Many can manage to deliver some successful projects, but if the overall customer experience does not meet (or exceed) expectations, then clients may rate the vendor unfavorably, forcing them to think about the real impact that such reviews will have in the success of the company down the road.

Inevitably, businesses that operate under these conditions will suffer and organizations will have to explain why they have lost so much market share. Seldom will they realize that the problem started many years ago, when companies paid bonuses and issued press releases to announce the quarterly or yearly results.

We need more professionals working towards achieving sustainable results that will reward the company for many years to come; and we need more corporations willing to align compensation and incentive packages that promote the right balance between short and long-term behavior.

Reward what you expect

This book is about PMs and project teams up-selling their company's products and services, exceeding customers' expectations, wowing them with every action, and impressing them with every effort to ensure their project is a success. The most successful project managers are capable of creating a team atmosphere where every day activity is conducive to either the success of the project at hand or the future relationship with the same customer.

In this environment, nothing else matters, except customer success, which ultimately and inevitably will translate into corporate success. I have had the pleasure of meeting and interacting with a few organization leaders that promote and reward a true customer-centric environment, and it is gratifying to see that more and more companies are embracing this 21st Century vision and management strategy every day.

In a perfect world, companies should provide incentives for executives, PMs, and employees in general to spend at least 60% of their time building the future customer base of the company, while the other 40% is spent in closing short-term business opportunities and delivering successful projects. When companies promote the opposite behavior, we observe a greater tendency for failing figures, unrealistic goals, frustrated employees, and dissatisfied customers (and shareholders).

Business leaders have the responsibility of transforming their company business strategies, challenging the status quo and the old cliché business models in order to find the most effective way of delivering value to shareholders, employees, and customers. Running a successful company is truly an art, and therefore it is all about creativity, open minds, breaking old paradigms, and finding new ways for achieving great results.

C-level executives should introduce more artful concepts in their daily management style, allowing for environments conducive to great discoveries and unrestrained thinking that creates unprecedented ideas that drive unparalleled results. Now that deserves rewards!

It is important to touch on the project managers' incentive models too. This book is about transforming PMs into active players in the business development process and as such, their compensation plans should be properly aligned not only with the expected goals of delivering successful and profitable projects for the corporation, but also with objectives such as:

- Customer success (aka customer satisfaction)
- Repeat-business (this is different than change-order business)
- Direct future business
- Referrals

Compensation experts say that for incentives to be effective companies must condition them to clear and measureable results. Project managers are evaluated best in a 360-degree format, utilizing a balanced scorecard system.

Inviting customers to provide honest and timely feedback on the performance of project managers and project teams is perhaps the best way to learn how they are perceived by the very people they serve.

Questionnaires should be brief and to the point, with clear and direct questions about the PM's and technical team performances. Often customers have difficulty finding the time to answer written surveys. A quick phone call from a VP or Director is all it takes to get the necessary answers to understand how the customer perceives the team.

It is extremely important to ask the customer for timely and constructive feedback to help the performance of our teams, as a way to ensure a successful project. Therefore, I strongly recommend performing feedback surveys not only after projects are complete, but also during their execution. Only then management will have an opportunity to provide PMs and technical team members with a prompt view of how they are being perceived by the customer.

Questions that should never be absent from a performance survey are:

- How would you rate our PM's integrity level?
- Would you recommend our PM to one of your colleagues in the industry?
- Would you recommend our company?
- What would you change in the team structure we currently have in place for your project?
- Do you feel comfortable dealing with our PM and team members?
- Are you satisfied with the value you are receiving?

Change order business

We should understand basic or traditional change order business as the legitimate scope adjustment required for the successful completion of the project, as openly and willingly agreed to by both customer and vendor. Scope change can take the form of scope increase, scope decrease, or simply scope modification.

Advanced repeat business practice—on the other hand—is the PM's ability to identify customers' *desires* or *wishes*, transform them into *needs*, and capitalize on those to generate more business. This is what we have called *Need Creation* in an earlier chapter. Project managers have the best position to identify pockets for repeat business opportunities than anyone else in the organization, including salespeople. They know the customer better than anybody else and more importantly, they spend more time before the customer than anybody else does, which also means they (should) have the customer's *trust*.

Project managers are also in the best position to identify elements that the sales team missed in the project's original scope. They can make suggestions to the customer on how to improve the final performance of the complete solution. They can recommend, for example, the replacement of components with better and more efficient ones, configuring some elements differently, removing unnecessary parts, and adding new features to enhance the overall functionality, quality, reliability, efficiency, longevity, and performance of the solution.

PMs and technical experts can very quickly create need for new or upgraded features where nobody else can. If done correctly and professionally, this can quickly translate into revenue generation. We already said that the key to repeat business is advocacy, which can only develop from a solid foundation of trust and integrity.

If we unnecessarily try to squeeze our customers for every possible drop of scope change business, we are destroying our own credibility and reputation, showing that our integrity pillars are weak, and ultimately removing any trust that may have previously existed between the customer and us. In other words, we are asking our customer never to come back and not to recommend our company and our people to anyone, ever.

Creating need for the purpose of deriving more revenue for the corporation must be done carefully, professionally, and with the highest levels of integrity. Only then will we assure the desired outcome, keeping a highly satisfied customer, and protecting the reputation of our company and that of ourselves.

Remember, the ultimate goal is advocacy and having a customer that returns for more is a good sign; having a customer that recommends our business to others is success.

The true secret to market dominance is not to sell more, but to never forget we are not alone and that competitors are always there working diligently to try to erode our market position. Our job (CEOs, VPs, PMs, Sales, and every single member of the organization) is to do everything in our power to prevent competitors from taking our customers. If we do this right, orders will come, revenue and profits will flow, and we will deliver value to our customers, shareholders, and employees; and inevitably, our business will flourish.

For this model to work we must never forget that we get what we reward, and therefore companies must offer project managers the correct incentives to achieve the desired results. If corporations do not break free from traditional and worn PM performance appraisal and reward models, companies will never achieve the goal of competitor isolation and market growth. Unconventional Project Managers work hard for the company's success and organizations must put in place proper incentives to compensate their contribution.

Project managers' incentives must be aligned with customer success, ethical revenue generation (change orders), and new business development (understood as new orders beyond existing projects).

Only when recognition and reward for these types of behavior are in place, will project managers start to transform the future of the organization.

One last key element that deserves clarification is that no matter how important or strategic the customer is, or how big or complex the new business opportunity the project manager was able to create or identify, the sales team should never take over the responsibility of closing the business. The PM must remain the key and primary point of interaction with the customer (remember *Trust*) and the Account or Sales Manager must remain behind the scenes, supporting the efforts of the PM and technical experts as needed.

Management and executives must have the ability to empower project managers to follow through and finish what they started. If they were able to transform a wish into need, or identify a unique new business opportunity, they deserve the right to close the deal. Perhaps they might need support and coaching from others in the organization, but if this is not to be the last time a PM brings in new business, he or she must be the one completing the closing process, and the company must reward him or her accordingly.

Chapter 21

Smart Account Management

Though this book is not about sales (at least not in the traditional sense) I think it is important to briefly discuss the aspect of account management, as it does play an important role in the revenue-generating process, regardless of who is executing it. In fact, I firmly believe that project managers are the ones that can best practice progressive account management. Let us analyze why:

We have already established that solid relationships with our clients should be at the base of business—especially repeat business. Does this mean that we have to go through the agonizing process of creating an account plan for all clients before we can build a good relationship with them? –Not necessarily.

Let's be honest, nobody likes to go through the painful trouble of creating a document we are not even sure is useful in the first place. Not even salespeople enjoy having to comply with such corporate and unnecessary practice. It seems redundant to do so since we all know in our heads what we need to do in order to secure orders from a particular customer.

Nevertheless, true account management serves a few very valuable purposes, some of which may not seem so obvious even to the most seasoned sales professional. First, account plans do not have to be extensive documents. In fact, studies demonstrate that the simpler and the shorter the document, the easier it is to write and maintain, and the more effective and useful it is for everybody in the organization.

There are hundreds, perhaps thousands of AP templates out there. My advice is to find a few reasonable ones and take the best from them to create a unique model that works for you and your company. Again, keep it brief, simple, and meaningful.

The importance of account planning lies on the very exercise of writing it. A good AP template should force us to do our homework and find out important and useful facts about our client or prospective buyer. It should have at least three key sections and contain the following information:

Section A – Basic Data & Intelligence

- Company size (in terms of people, revenue, and profitability)
- Main and secondary lines of business (how they make their money)
- Mergers & Acquisitions (timeline of who bought who)
- Who their customers are
- What geographies they serve
- Who their competitors are
- Their organizational map
  o Which individuals have the power to make purchasing decisions
  o Who is in a position to influence those decisions
  o Who can advocate or champion for us
  o Who can oppose us in winning the project
  o Who are the end users
- Contact information for all of the above (email and phone numbers)
- Personality profile for all of the above (friendliness, hobbies & pastimes, birthday date, accessibility, favorite food and restaurant, spouse name, dreams & wishes, problems & frustrations, opinion about our company and products/ services, etc.).

Section B - Strategy

- A detail description of our Capture Strategy
    - o Long-Term Account Management Strategy (do not focus on specific opportunities)
    - o Short-Term Account Management Strategy (how to secure next order)
    - o Resources needed
    - o Time & Event Strategy (who goes before the client and when)
    - o Competitor Analysis (who they are. Include SWOT table)

Section C – Execution

- Execution Plan
    - o Schedule (do what, when. Include phone calls, meetings, demos, seminars, meals, golf outings, etc.)
- Tracking Table
    - o A simple table (in Excel) that serves the purpose of keeping track of every action we have taken, including things like phone calls, meetings, meal meetings, trips, presentations, trade shows, technical seminars, conference calls, golf games, etc. Every interaction with the customer must be recorded and time-stamped. This helps you remember what you have done, especially when reporting to your manager or handing over the account to another person.

This type of Account Plan is by definition dynamic, which forces you to keep updating it every time you interact with the customer. This is the way all account plans should be, for customer organizations are not static at all.

Additionally, there is another very good reason for creating good, sound account plans. Our own organizations are not static either and we are all constantly moving around. A well-maintained account plan makes it very easy to pass a client onto somebody else when we are moving on. Everything there is to know about a client—including every interaction we had with them—is in the document, so anyone can easily jump-in and get a head start to continue the execution of the Account Strategy.

This becomes particularly valuable when an Account is moved between PMs and the Sales Team, for example. In organizations that truly embrace and promote the role of the project manager as a revenue-generating agent, it is not rare to have clients moved between Sales and Project Teams, and more importantly, both groups must have access to review and update the account plan in real time.

Project managers spend a considerable amount of time with clients during project execution. This is the perfect opportunity to gather necessary data to complete Section A of the Account Plan. Information in this section alone is extremely valuable for the long-term, as some of it is very difficult to obtain, like the role of each participating team member and their attitude towards our company and our competitors.

PMs have privileged access to this kind of information, as it they can gather it casually and slowly over time. Salespeople only have a few meeting opportunities to find out everything there is about a particular client. PMs, on the other hand, have every opportunity to casually interact with their counterparts and learn the most relevant aspects of customers and their organizations, without being intrusive.

I have been astonished to observe companies with very poor knowledge of their customers. Complete sales teams are struggling to get more time in front of clients to pitch their product, literally combing the Internet in search of customer data; all the while, the project team is busy on another floor, building a solution for the same client, and meeting with them on a weekly basis. I simply do not get it.

Often project and sales teams are in different floors, sometimes in different buildings, or cities, even different countries, but the information is closer than you think. Usually project managers have valuable insight about the customer's organization than salespeople do, and when that is not the case, PMs can very easily access the customer for the intelligence the team requires.

Working in silos does not help the bottom line; that is a fact. So, why do companies insist on separating the two most important elements of the repeat business equation? The closer sales and project teams are the better for the organization, for there has to be a natural, friendly, open, and cooperative communication between these two traditionally rival groups.

Building a wall between those that sell products or solutions to customers and those who deliver them is perhaps the biggest act of self-sabotage an organization can commit. Bringing them together and having them working together towards the common goal of securing the next order for the company is the key to continued growth.

By implementing this model, we can completely remove from the discussion familiar statements such as:

- *"The sales guys completely undersold this project. It's going to be in the red in no time."*
- *"It's going to be impossible to deliver this project on time. There are not enough hours even to design the solution, let alone building it."*
- *"These project people, no matter how many hours we give them, it is never enough."*
- *"Engineering is always sandbagging their project estimations, making us the most expensive vendor out there. At this rate we will not be able to book any more projects."*

Capture teams

Selling in a project environment should be a team effort where not only critical information and intelligence is shared, but where a common strategy is defined to manage each account. This is why I talk about *Capture Teams* instead of *Sales Teams*. A sales team is composed of salespeople only, while a capture team is formed by a variety of different players, including sales, PMs, engineers and technicians, executives, marketing, external agents and integrators, subject matter experts, etc.

Given the dynamic nature of the account plan and considering that multiple people are part of the *capture team* responsible for developing the account, I highly recommend account plan documents to reside on a shared server or the *Cloud*, where anyone *touching* the account can access and update them easily.

This live document must reflect accurately and timely any changes on the client side. If a key member of the customer team changes positions or leaves the company, the account plan must promptly reflect this event. If not all stakeholders in the organization interacting with the customer do this, the account plan becomes easily obsolete and therefore useless.

If your company does not promote the use of account plans, or if they are not serving their purpose, I encourage you to take the initiative to start showing your colleagues the true value behind such a simple document. Make sure it does not contain unnecessary information and make sure it is accessible by all and kept up to date in nearly real time.

Show the document in strategy meetings, prove its real value by highlighting relevant information, draw relationship maps that show how different players in the client's organization interact with each other and the effect those interactions have on your company's ability to book orders. This simple exercise will separate you from your peers, making you a unique contributor in your organization, catapulting you to a much more successful and rewarding career.

Chapter 22

The Chicken or The Egg?

People often ask me how project managers can get to play a significant role in the revenue-generating process if the company is still struggling to secure the first contract with a client. This is a very good question and I can easily answer it using the chicken or the egg metaphor.

In a perfect world companies would be able to secure the first project with a particular customer without major obstacles, so then the PM and project team can devote their time to building whatever it is the company sold, plus executing some of the concepts I have presented in this book to pave the road for future business.

However, the question is why would a company that had no major issues securing the first piece of business need a different strategy to continue to drive repeat business from the same client? The answer to this question has two parts:

1. First, when corporations believe that simply because they had not major difficulties securing the first project they will have similar results when competing for the next order, trouble truly begins.

   Repeat business is by definition difficult business (I often say) because whatever tactics salespeople used to win the first project will not be as effective once the customer has had the experience of working with your company's delivery team. If your project team is not able to impress the customer in the process, things can go south very rapidly.

Promises will no longer count, as now the customer knows firsthand what the PM and project team are capable of, and more importantly, what they are not. Unless your team did an excellent job at building and delivering the project, or your company is in a monopoly situation, the sales team is going to have a very difficult time convincing the customer to award a second contract.

The most successful companies on the planet ask themselves this very question the moment they receive the first project and immediately design a strategy to secure the next piece of business. The company never leaves project execution to chance and the employees do everything in their power to ensure an amazing project execution experience for the customer. Successful corporations never treat the sales process as a repeatable formula, since they know the second sell is always more difficult than the first.

The trick is in having a repeat business culture in the organization, where everybody that interacts with customers—including project managers, technical, and service teams—are trained to embrace their role in the revenue-generating process. Everything that we have covered in this book suddenly becomes relevant, since now the PM can put all these concepts to work to not only ensure a successful project for both the customer and the company, but also to ensure that every action is always taken with the next order in mind.

If my readers could engrave this concept alone in their minds, I would feel I have accomplished the objective of writing this book. Winning a project is easy; getting the next one is the difficult part; and we have to help our sales teams accomplish our common goal.

2. However, the first point assumes the company has been successful in securing the first order, and often the argument is that competition is so fierce that winning the first project proves to be challenging, to say the least. In some cases (like when penetrating new markets, for example) getting that first contract may be more difficult than expected, and here lies the real power of the PM's role in sales:

It is not a rare practice to lower margin expectations in order to secure the first project in a new market or untapped territory. Most companies in the world use this tactic to remove entry barriers, but then fail to deliver new orders. Now we know why this happens and are better equipped to prevent the same from happening to our organizations.

I call this strategy *spearheading* or *seeding*. The initial investment on the first job is all we need to unleash the true power of our project managers and technical teams to deliver outstanding value to the customer. The objective is to build a successful project (the way the customer defines it), and give the client every reason to come back for more and recommend our products, solutions, people, and company to others.

Your CEO and executive team will do everything in their power to secure that first project, and will often succeed, but sustainable business depends tremendously on your ability to deliver a successful project experience to the customer, one that is so impressive they will not hesitate for a moment to come back for more.

Without a successful project implementation (again, the way the customer defines success), the spearheading effort will go to waste, as that will be the first and last project your company will ever win with that customer. When entering new niches, markets, or territories, this is even more important, as failure to deliver a successful project to one customer can easily mean a rejection by the entire industry in that region.

Do you want fries with your order?

So what came first, the chicken or the egg? —For the purpose of our analysis it does not matter much, for the strategy to secure repeat business does not change. Whether it was easy for your company to secure the first project or not, the role of the PM continues to be essential in the continued success of the corporation with that particular customer and those around them.

The important thing to remember is that no matter what, we must always do everything in our power to impress our customer. That is the only effective way to isolate our company from competition and protect our accounts. Project performance is necessary, but always putting the way the customer measures performance first; going the extra mile and finding every opportunity to help our client with answers, information, and knowledge.

Buying the customer dinner or delivering a compliant project is not enough anymore, as now customers are looking for unique value, for that *wow* factor that only very few can deliver. The call is to under-commit and over-achieve every time, to deliver value beyond expectations, to make the customer feel special, and convince them that no other vendor will be able to deliver to the same standards, regardless of price or company size.

Therefore, whenever you find yourself wondering whether the chicken or the egg came first, do not spend too much time trying to find the answer and just make sure you always *deliver fries with that order*—as my friend Paul Tildsley likes to say—, whether they asked for them or not. Get the customer more than they expect, and start driving quality repeat-business for your organization.

Chapter 23

Dealing With Difficult Customers

I am almost certain that most of us have had the experience of dealing with a difficult customer at some point in our careers. I am also sure that those who were on the other side of the table have perceived some of us as being a difficult customer at least once.

What is the realistic definition of a difficult customer? What makes them difficult? How should we react to a demanding client?

A difficult customer is simply a person or group of people that have a very clear understanding of what they want (in terms of what they are buying) and are not prepared to accept any mistakes, shortfalls, delays, unpleasant surprises, or anything that jeopardizes the success of their project or buying experience.

Often we perceive difficult customers as being demanding, unapproachable, unreasonable, unwilling to compromise, negative, condescending, intolerant, narrow-minded, overconfident, and at times even disrespectful. In this chapter we are going to analyze the psychology of difficult customers, so that we can better understand them, deal with them, and ultimately turn them into satisfied, advocating clients; and why not, allies and even friends.

Think of one of your current customers, anyone (it does not have to be a difficult one). Put yourself in his or her shoes; see the world from their eyes. A difficult customer is simply a regular customer who grew tired of frustrating buying experiences. Difficult customers are just people who have been *burned* multiple times before by negligent vendors or customer service people.

I strongly believe a difficult customer is simply the result of bad service. If the customer experience is always outstanding, then there will be no difficult customers. However, companies today insist in treating customers poorly, under-delivering, underperforming, and always disappointing those who entrusted us with the success of their own projects.

It is in our nature to under-deliver; we always come short on almost everything we do. In sports, our team *almost* won the championship, in the last golf tournament, we *almost* shot par, or we were *almost* on time for our meeting. We are always *almost* there. When we take our families on vacation, we always spend more than budgeted and usually *almost* missed the flight. When we go grocery shopping and are about to check out a text message arrives telling us not to forget the milk, and we always react with the typical *"Oops, I almost forgot"* apologetic answer.

If we are always short on most things we attempt, why do we always plan and prepare for the exact desired goal and never beyond that mark? If all we need is a B to pass the course, then we prepare ourselves to get a B. What happens 90% of the time? –The exam was harder than expected and we get a C. We should have studied harder as if what we needed was an A.

If our doctor's appointment is at 9:00 am, we plan our morning routine as if everything will happen according to plan, so we arrive just in time for our appointment. What happens 90% of the time? –The bread gets burned, the phone rings, we do not know what to wear, we take longer in the shower, the traffic is worse than expected, or there was an accident on the road, we forgot to Google the address and got lost, etc. In the end 90% of the time, we are late.

What we should have done is plan for the worst and hope for the best. By simply assuming that at least some of all those unplanned events will happen, we would have set the alarm clock 30 minutes earlier and our arrival would have been prompt.

In the project world, it is almost impossible to impress our customers if we always plan to <u>meet</u> the contractual obligations. If the objective is to build a new soccer stadium for the next world cup, we have a very clear deadline to meet, one that is obviously non-negotiable. What do we do 90% of the time? —We plan and budget our project to have the stadium ready <u>in time</u> for the event; and that is precisely where the problem is.

Skilled project managers always plan for the worst and work for the best. They always under-promise and end up over-achieving, impressing, wowing customers. They know that a smooth project is a fallacy and that teams will miss deadlines and budgets. What do they do? —They plan and run the project as if the deadline was two or four months earlier and define appropriate incentives for team members and suppliers to achieve that goal. When something goes wrong, delays affect the project, they even miss the new aggressive deadline, but thanks to this strategy, they still manage to complete the project in time for world-cup inauguration day.

If we ask customers in any industry, they will tell us that their biggest frustration and disappointment is with late projects. As you see, it is very easy to turn a regular customer into one that feels dissatisfied. The challenge lies in turning that frustrated client into happy and loyal customer.

Some clients have dedicated their entire careers to supervising projects like the ones you have at hand today and if their experiences have not being positive, most likely we are facing a demanding customer from the start. Clients are under tremendous amounts of pressure to deliver successful projects, the same way we are. The only difference between them and us is the way each party understands success.

This is why I insist so much in making sure we build and deliver successful projects the way the <u>customer</u> defines them, not the way our companies do. If your client has not seen a successful project in a while, most likely you have the perfect recipe for a difficult customer. They cannot afford negligent mistakes anymore, nor are they looking forward to senseless excuses. They just need you, your team, and your company to <u>get the job done</u> correctly the first time.

Do not think for a moment that your customers do not accept mistakes. That is a misconception. Primarily customers are people, human beings that know very well that we all make honest mistakes and they are prepared to accept them adequately. What they will not tolerate (pardon my language) are *stupid* mistakes. Yes, those careless mistakes that we could have easily avoided if we were paying attention turn a reasonable customer into a difficult one very quickly.

Let us assume, for example, that you are at a restaurant with a group of friends or business associates. You call the waiter and ask for the menu and instead you get the wine list. Then you order a bottle of a good quality cabernet sauvignon and they bring it ice cold, as if it were white wine or champagne. Your friend ordered a medium-rare steak and instead she got a well-done cut. Eventually your sympathy for honest mistakes turns into frustration.

After dinner, you asked for the bill and you see charges for things you did not order. I know this is an extreme example, but I am sure most of you can relate to at least part of this or a similar situation. It is very difficult to keep your cool after a while and inevitably, we become a frustrated, disappointed client. In the waiter's eyes, we are just difficult customers.

However, often times when we are on the delivery side, we pay the price for someone else's mistakes, and we simply inherit a difficult customer without doing anything wrong. That is okay and quite common. Getting a difficult customer simply means some other vendor managed to ruin their customer experience, leaving you the empty road to impress this client and turn him or her into a loyal, advocating customer. The trick is to learn how to turn this apparent unfair event into a tremendous opportunity to impress this new client and turn him or her into the most loyal customer of all.

Here are the top five things you should invariably do when inheriting a difficult customer:

1. Focus all your energy on avoiding any careless mistakes. This will only put you on the same boat as their previous vendor (not a good place to be).
2. Quickly show them you are different. Act extremely professional, think like them, talk like them, act like them. Defend their position and play on their side.
3. Every day show your commitment to their success, not yours, nor your company's, but their success.
4. Always remember, they are tired of being disappointed. Show them that you are not up to disappointing them too. Your goal is to make them look successful in front of their bosses.
5. Do something for them to impress them as soon as possible, and repeat it every time you can.

Never forget that the difficult customer does not really exist. Instead, we have different types of clients. Some are capable of leaving past frustrating experiences behind and give new vendors the chance to prove themselves, while others cannot hide their frustrations and see every new vendor relationship as an inexorable repetition of past bad experiences.

It is ten times easier to turn a good, easy-going customer into a disappointed and frustrated one, than it is to turn a difficult client into a happy and satisfied individual. It takes a tremendous amount of effort and dedication to make unhappy customers stay, let alone change their opinion.

This is why we should focus all our energy into making first clients' impressions memorable and keeping happy customers satisfied, so we never have to waste time, energy, and resources trying to undo what we did wrong, and to convince frustrated customers to stay and give us another chance.

There is only one thing worse than having an unhappy customer, and that is having an unhappy customer who spreads the word about our flaws and mistakes in the entire marketplace.

What are the consequences of the above? We slowly but surely start to see declining sales and companies firing CEOs and VPs, replacing customer service and sales staff, even bringing new salespeople with impressive *Rolodexes* and resumes. However, these measures will have little to no effect on the company's revenue and bottom line figures, unless we deal with the problem at the root.

Penny wise, dollar foolish

We must fix the customer experience first, from sales to marketing and from project execution to service. We have to make the customer say the three-letter word: Wow! Until he or she does, we have not fixed the problem yet. We have to make this disappointed customer return, even if it means hitting the bottom line. Businesses that insist in saving a penny today instead of investing to regain a customer's trust are doomed. If you have been around for a while you have surely seen this; and if you are in the early stages of your career, trust me, you will see it.

Losing a client not only means losing an order or whatever number of orders this client could have given us over time, but it also means losing credibility in the marketplace. Corporations spend millions of dollars in advertising and marketing campaigns to convince the marketplace of their attributes (quality, values, great customer experience, etc.). However, they seem prepared to throw all that investment and efforts away by letting a frustrated customer go, so he or she can tell the entire world about how bad we are. It just does not make any sense!

Successful companies take this aspect very seriously and they truly embrace this theory. They clearly understand that the key to a successful business lies in three basic pillars:

1. Make customers happy;
2. Keep customers happy; and
3. If we made a mistake, do whatever it takes to fix the problem and keep that customer from leaving.

The project manager's role, when it comes to dealing with a difficult customer (*previously disappointed customer*), is to put the pages of this book to work, so that the customer can learn to trust again. It is like a healing process, it takes time, but if done patiently and persistently, people can again experience the joy of receiving the highest quality product and service, as well as the most successful project as a result.

Once again, PMs are in the best position to turn an unhappy client into a satisfied customer again, for they and the complete project team are the only ones tasked with building and delivering something of value for them. Not only the result must impress the client, the journey to that successful end must also be full of *wow* moments.

Unfortunately, corporations insist on sending salespeople to achieve the same. This is a fundamental mistake; salespeople do not offer value, project managers, project teams, and service professionals do.

We can send our best salespeople, VPs, even CEOs to try to convince a customer there is no reason to feel unhappy, because they are giving him or her their word that the problems will get fixed and will never happen again. But we easily forget that PMs and project teams are the ones with the mandate to work every day with that customer in solving issues, building trust, delivering value, and exceeding expectations, so that the customer can give our products, our team, and our company the highest ratings.

Only then, the customer is ready to do business with our company again, only then we can rest assured we have truly recovered a customer, one that is now ready to recommend our work to others again.

Chapter 24

The Law of Gravity

In this planet, nothing escapes the law of gravity, not even businesses. Literally thousands of companies of all sizes are surrounding us, all of them trying to go in one direction: Up.

Start-ups want to gain recognition as stable small companies. Small firms want to be medium size. Medium size businesses want join the select group of large corporations.

Very seldom do I see a company with a clear plan to maintain a steady horizontal course, not growing or downsizing. When a company decides it is time to downsize, it is usually because of their own failure to sustain continuous growth.

Physicists have always been in search for the answer for perpetual movement, but despite all efforts, objects will always stop moving unless new force is applied to them. Inexplicably business leaders insist on forcing their companies onto risky journeys in search of perpetual growth, defying the most basic law of physics.

When you throw a rock vertically up in the air the object will accelerate and climb until it runs out of energy, which is when it will start to fall back down to the ground. You can try as many times as you want, applying the biggest amount of force possible to launch the piece of rock up higher, but inevitably it will eventually slow down until it finds its optimal climbing point, before it starts its natural descend back to the ground.

The same laws apply in business. All companies need a certain amount of energy to launch, and most will succeed in their journey until their optimal performance point is about to be reached, which is when we observe deceleration, and later a reversal process that is characterized by decreased sales, profits, market share, etc.

This is when executives do not know what to do, stock prices fall, boards fire CEOs, and everybody tries to find a way to keep the momentum going. Remember this: It is naturally impossible.

The only way to achieve continuous growth is to re-inject energy to the corporation, which is usually done by adding capital, more customers organically, or through mergers and acquisitions. Business theory and history have proved that no company can achieve continuous growth without introducing at least one of these three components.

In my professional career, I have seen small companies experiment explosive growth like rockets traveling into space, and I have also witnessed very large multi-national corporations slow-down and crumble into pieces as the law of gravity brings them back to earth.

Why do we observe this obsession with an ever-growing company? —Some scholars indicate the answer lies in greed, while others prefer to offer much simpler explanations, such as that a company by definition is a growing entity, as growth is the only vehicle for bringing renewed value to shareholders, employees, and customers.

However, what does growth and gravity have to do with project managers, revenue generation, and customer service? —Achieving growth means a certain level of success, which often drives an arrogant behavior in some people, which can easily permeate into a company's brand and image.

We have already discussed that climbing to a number one position in business is the easy part of the journey and that staying there is the challenge. The world looks significantly better—or at least different—from the top, and companies can easily forget that staying at the top takes far more work than it took them to get there.

When corporations are thriving, they often fail to recognize that it is then that they need to revisit marketing strategies to strengthen and protect their brand(s). It is then that corporate leaders must assume the humblest of positions towards the marketplace. During the stages of growth, companies need to design new strategies to find the necessary energy to continue to climb (defying the law of gravity) or find the optimal point to remain performing at their best.

Unfortunately, the opposite occurs and corporations more often than not fall victims to their own success (weight). When products or brands achieve high success levels, corporations tend to believe that the marketplace will respond with perpetual loyalty, so there is no need to pay much attention to project and customer success. The laws of physics also apply here, as clients slowly but surely begin to depart the group of once satisfied customers.

One size does not fit all

In a similar manner, strong branded companies can make the mistake of relaxing their market penetration strategies, especially if the brand is stronger in one side of the business, but not necessarily in others. One size does not fit all in this case, and brand rejection is not a rare occurrence in business, especially when companies want to enter a new niche using the brand strength achieved in a different segment.

Companies that overplay the merger and acquisition card to deliver growth, for example, will eventually face this phenomenon, especially when the segments or niches are completely distant from the core competencies for which the company and the brand are recognized in the marketplace. Being the best in one area does not necessarily give a company the authority to expect an easy ride in a different niche.

- *"We are ACME Computers; customers would be crazy not to buy pianos with the ACME name on them…"*

- *"We have successfully built more than a thousand bridges around the world; NASA should have no problems trusting us with their next expedition to Mars…"*

The world of mergers and acquisitions is the ideal scenario for situations like these. The pressure for continuous growth is such, that some companies acquire unrelated businesses with the sole objective of growing revenue numbers.

I am not against diversification at all, as there is where the key to long-term sustainability is, but rebranding (absorbing) a company and its products is the most egocentric corporate act there is, one that often produces devastating effects.

Here is an example. If a well-known car manufacturing company decides to acquire the most recognized computer corporation in the world, it makes no sense for the new owner to rename the acquired company and computer brand to reflect the brand of the cars they make.

It is an extreme example, I know, but if you look around your industry, you will start to realize there are several examples where this is precisely what companies have done. As a result, sales decline, business shrinks, workers lose their jobs, and ultimately the acquired business is either close-down or sold.

Being at the top of a market niche at times feels like being in a monopoly situation, as often our products completely dominate the market segment. However, in a free market based economy, monopolies do not exist and competition is king. Your company's closest competitors and those that follow behind them, are spending every dollar they can in order to displace your company from the dominant position. Unless your company does something creative quick, your competitors will succeed. It is not a matter of if they do it, but when they will overtake your company's number one place.

Hassle-free returns

When flying high in the marketplace it is very easy to let the guard down, relaxing the strict customer success rules that brought our company to the preferred spot in the first place. Some years ago, a competitor of a strong retail brand invented the *hassle-free returns* concept and quickly took the number one place. Now the no questions asked approach to returning consumer products is the norm in the marketplace and any other practice simply means frustrated customers going to the competition.

Customer service is not (cannot be) a department or a phone number. Customer service is a philosophy, a way of living, and a dogma. This is why I call it *Customer Success* instead. For it to work, all levels of the corporation must exercise customer service, from the CEO to the person that answers the phone. Project managers, service professionals, and project execution teams have a tremendous responsibility in injecting renewed energy into this corporate rocket, so it continues to thrive, defying the law of gravity at all times.

Anybody interacting with customers or potential clients must be fully trained in the corporate customer success philosophy, understand it, embrace it, and execute it brilliantly. Whether people interact in person with clients, on the phone, or on the Web, customer success must always be at the top of the priority list. Any other model that does not consistently embrace this principle will most likely fail.

When employees are interacting with a customer or prospective client, they must dedicate their full attention to that client exclusively; absolutely no interruptions allowed. Almost every time I approach a hotel reception desk, the same most basic customer service rule is broken. In the middle of my conversation with the front desk person, the phone rings and he or she does not hesitate for a second to pick it up promptly.

To my astonishment, not only the representative answers the phone in the middle of my own customer service experience, but also the attention shifts completely from me to the other client several floors above the lobby. Even more surprising is the fact that no matter how many calls may come through during my interaction with the employee, he or she will always answer the phone and give the other client his or her full attention, forcing me to gaze at the ceiling or pretend I am reading an email on my smart phone while I wait.

Why do I have to wait? —I was there first and I was already receiving service. Why would the employee shift the attention from me to another client? Just to clarify, I am talking about well-recognized five-star hotel brands.

One day I decided to express my disappointment with the practice and told the front desk person that her action was equivalent to letting another person cut (physically) in front of me at the front desk line. Her explanation was that it was corporate policy to answer the phones promptly at all times.

I have been traveling internationally for almost 20 years, and no matter where I go I always observe this behavior. In some cases, the employee interrupts the discussion with me to answer the phone, but at least asks the other person to hold the line, and she continues servicing my request.

Given the massive number of calls that come to hotel reception desks, I have yet to understand why hotel companies do not have operators exclusively dedicated to answering customers' calls and attending to their requests. Some companies do have a switchboard service, but when clients ask for the reception desk they simply comply and put the call through. In my opinion, hotels should have two teams of reception desk representatives: Those who serve customers face to face, and those who serve them over the phone.

Having one doing both inevitably creates a frustrating customer experience, not only for the customer down in the lobby, but also for the client up in a room, forced to hold the line because the front desk representative is serving a customer downstairs. They both demand and deserve attention, and they both want it now; why should one have to wait?

Project managers, service, and technical teams spend considerable amounts of time interacting with clients. It is their job to make every experience memorable and to give that customer absolutely no reason to feel the need to go to the competition. This is what companies require to continue to thrive and climb higher in their journey for success.

Chapter 25

The Project Sales Process

Traditionally members of the sales team execute sales cycles much in isolation from the rest of the organization. This practice has rapidly evolved into a more collaborative approach whereby project managers, engineers, and technicians work together as a team with account managers and other members of the sales group.

This natural evolution has taken place mainly because of either undersold or poorly executed projects. The blaming exercises observed in the corporation when projects did not deliver the expected results, stemmed the realization that both, sales and execution teams needed to work together in order to increase the quality and accuracy of the bids submitted.

In my opinion, this is the only way to ensure successful project execution and avoid internal confrontation and unnecessary *finger-pointing* scenes when bad results occur.

The modern sales process blends the traditional sales and execution phases into a single project workflow, now simply known as *the project*. The entire process has three very distinct phases:

1. Pre-acquisition
2. Acquisition
3. Execution

Pre-acquisition

Every activity that the organization carries out in order to identify a business opportunity creates need for a project and creates preference for the company, its products, and services. The ultimate goal of the pre-acquisition phase is to obtain an invitation to submit a bid, or better yet, to be single-sourced to supply the product or solution for the customer.

Once the team receives the request for proposal it needs to decide whether to proceed to the next phase or not. This is the *Go/No-Go Gate*. Usually, the sales or account manager makes this simple and quick decision.

It is important to keep in mind that project managers and service managers can easily play the role of account managers as well. In essence, whoever is closest to the account (the customer) should be the Account Manager.

Acquisition

In this phase, the team will focus on analyzing the RFQ and technical specifications supplied by the client, performing detail risk analysis, and mitigation planning. The team will also perform a quick assessment of the effort required to successfully build and deliver the project. All this information is then used to cross the next gate, which is known as the *Bid/No-Bid Gate*.

This gate is a more formal approval process that involves the preparation of several reports and the presentation of the project opportunity and risk mitigation plan to the approval committee, usually conformed by senior management representatives.

If the capture team obtains approval to submit a bid, then they will concentrate on preparing the complete proposal, including execution plans, schedule, organization charts, and a detail description of the proposed execution strategy for the entire project.

Different team members and other resources will work on different sections of the RFQ, carefully responding to every aspect, including technical, commercial, and legal details.

The team also performs thorough requirement analysis in order to estimate the materials and effort needed to successfully build and deliver the project to the client, including warranty and service phases. This analysis is critical, as it is here where pricing is traditionally determined (refer to the chapter on pricing models).

Upon approval, the team submits the bid to the customer for consideration. If the company secures the order, the project is booked and moves onto the next phase.

Execution

After award, the project is handed-over to the execution team under the direction of the project manager. Key steps in this phase include scope clarification, planning, purchasing, development, shipping, installation, commissioning, testing, acceptance, and warranty.

Since my readers are mostly project managers and project professionals, I am not going to describe in more detail the steps of this execution phase, as I expect those to be core competencies of my audience.

The modern project sales process breaks the walls that traditionally existed between the sales and execution functions, blending them into a single project stream. Under this new model, roles and responsibilities are also combined, which naturally creates the space necessary for the early involvement of project managers in the pre-acquisition and acquisition phases (Sales), while at the same time allowing for the continuous involvement of sales or account managers in the project execution and service phases.

This blended project team is often known as *Business Pursuit Team* or simply *Capture Team*, terms that clearly describe the function and ultimate goal of every team member: To capture the business opportunity and transform it into a successful project for both, the company and the customer.

The sole presence of the project manager in the very early stages of the project pursuit is fundamental in achieving key common objectives, such as:

- Execution team buy-in.
- Solidarity when performing effort estimations.
- Project scope understanding.
- Early introduction of PM to customer (*Trust*).
- Sense of pride and ownership in the acquisition phase.

Similarly, the sole presence of the sales or account manager throughout the execution phase guarantees the project team a sense of commitment in the complete success of the project, which ultimately results in high customer satisfaction levels, which in turn signifies increased chances for repeat business.

The following diagram outlines the workflow discussed in this chapter:

Project Workflow

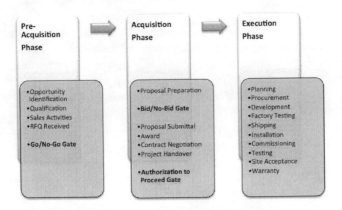

Chapter 26

The Power of Technical Seminars

In the pages of this book, we have studied the importance of marketing elements such as branding. We have also analyzed the typical sales process and the drivers that motivate customers to buy. One of the most difficult barriers to overcome is the potential client's reluctance to listen to a salesperson's pitch. The most conservative studies show that the salespeople's biggest frustration is customers closing the door on them even before they get an opportunity to present their products or services.

You may or may not have realized this, but trade shows are a response to this very problem. These fairs offer the right environment for potential clients and vendors to be together on a common floor for a few days, sharing ideas, challenges, wishes, dreams, and desires (see chapter on Create Need). The fair is also an opportunity for vendors to display their products, companies, and best practices.

I hate to insist on the same concept once again, but salespeople are not well positioned to break through a door that is already shut. Many companies question the value of trade shows because they do not draw any orders from the fairs, and often they decide to exclude themselves from such events for that reason.

It is important to remember that trade shows are not sales events; they are marketing fairs, an opportunity to strengthen the brand, to introduce a product, or to highlight certain expertise. More fundamentally, a trade show is a place for vendors and customers to meet.

It is disappointing to see the important number of companies paying significant amounts of money to have a booth at an industry trade show, only to pass on the opportunity to present a technical paper during the event. Whenever I try to find an answer to this situation, I hear one of three reasons:

1. They do not allow us to mention our products.

2. Competitors will be in the audience.

3. We are too late to prepare and submit a paper before the deadline.

The truth to the matter is that, for the most part, corporations are not taking this very seriously; otherwise, there should always be a technical paper ready for submittal to an industry trade show or conference. After all, companies are (or want to be) the subject matter experts in the core technologies, knowledge, or skills they are selling.

Trade show and conference dates are published with sufficient time in advance for all vendors to have a fair chance at submitting their papers for review, so time to prepare and submit the material should never be an issue or excuse not to leverage the tremendous brand positioning opportunities that trade shows and conferences offer.

As I mentioned before, trade shows are not sales events, but an opportunity to connect with our target audience and position our brand(s). There is no need to mention our products during a technical paper presentation, because the only objective is to position our company brand and our people as the experts in the field. Products can be demonstrated on the show floor.

Let us not fool ourselves; competitors will always be following what our company does. Market intelligence is a fact in business life and your company should be playing the game as much as your competitors do.

Attending other vendors' presentations, visiting their booths, studying their products and service models, buying and testing their products, and evaluating their pricing schemes as well as marketing and branding strategies should be at the top of your company's priorities. Any company ignoring these basic business practices has no right to complain for declining sales or market erosion.

Now let us talk about cost. Companies usually have a difficult time justifying the expense of participating in industry trade shows, a decision that should be at the top of their priority list, as these are perhaps the best opportunity to strengthen the position of a brand. Much like in the case of not training people for the fear of them leaving, excluding ourselves from relevant events such as trade shows and industry conferences can hurt the company significantly, far beyond the mere cost of participation.

Similarly, technical presentations, panel discussions, and forum moderation opportunities should be at the top of the priority list when it comes to marketing spending. Having a booth should always be secondary, never the other way around. Do not get me wrong, booth space is important and should always be consistent with the size and image of the company, but the highest ROI is not in the booth itself, but in everything else that happens during the show.

As a project manager and leader of subject matter experts, it is your job and responsibility to encourage people in your organization to write and present papers at trade shows and congress events. Remember, the main objective of these activities is not to highlight your products, services, or technologies. Instead, the main goal is to contribute to the successful execution of your company branding strategy. Yes, it is not about what your company makes and sells, it is about the people and their expertise; it is about positioning and strengthening your company's brand.

Sometimes it is more difficult to understand the benefit of being there than the damage of actually not being there at all.

If your company decides to skip a trade show altogether and not even present a technical paper, the message you are sending to the marketplace is that you do not care enough about customers and potential clients. It gives the impression that your company is not committed to solving the market's most important problems, and that your corporation only appears in the scene when there is money to be made. Customers dislike this behavior very much, and yes, they notice it.

A different alternative

Nonetheless, there is an alternative to traditional and crowded trade shows. If keeping your competitors at bay and intimacy are your concerns, entertain the idea of delivering personalized and private technical seminars. I have used this tactic very successfully throughout my career and have found that very seldom will a customer close the door to an opportunity to listen to the latest findings in a certain technical area or product development.

Find an engaging theme, like *Technology Day*, *Customer Day*, *Knowledge Transfer Seminar*, or anything that your market intelligence indicates will trigger your client's interest. Then ask the potential client for a meeting to discuss the event and the topics that may or may not be of their interest.

If you encounter resistance to the idea, it never fails to explain that this is part of an industry series event and that other potential clients (your client's competitors) have already benefited from listening to your material. The key is to secure your potential client's attendance to a privately held event that offers value, such as a *lunch and learn*, technical seminar, technology day, or whatever name you want use.

The technical topic must be appealing and completely absent of sales messages. The audience must feel at ease in a purely technical environment where the main driver is a learning experience and a desire to share acquired knowledge and practices.

This type of event can take place in your client's offices or in a neutral place, like a hotel meeting facility nearby. You should never host these events in your own offices, unless necessary due to demonstration or facility touring reasons, which can always take place separately.

In my own experience early Monday mornings work best, since customers are just returning from a well-deserved weekend break and have had no chance to start the week yet. Book the seminar with enough notice, so that they can schedule other commitments adequately around your event.

These technical seminars are, in my opinion, one of the best and most effective sales and marketing tools a company can utilize. They are also efficient, since the cost is limited to the organization of a private event targeted to a very specific audience and for a brief amount of time, usually not more than half a day. Additionally, your clients will give you their full attention, since nobody is presenting other papers at the same time, which is always the case at trade shows and industry conferences.

Your marketing department can get creative with this tool and mix it with a customer entertainment event, such as a golf tournament or clinic, or a more formal lunch or dinner afterwards. The important aspect here is to obtain the client's full attention, and ultimately their business and loyalty.

Once again, it is not about your products or services, but the problems your customers are facing today, the emerging technologies or techniques for solving them, and the unique know-how and expertise your team has in implementing successful projects that can effectively address those issues.

Chapter 27

Assumptions

Almost two decades ago, I heard a personal coach say a phrase that I engraved in my head forever. His name is Brian Tracy, and he said, *"Incorrect assumptions lie at the root of every failure. Have the courage to test your assumptions."* Since that day, I have encountered numerous occasions to apply the lesson of such simple sentence.

It is incredible, but in our personal lives, we face countless situations where our own assumptions have led us to tremendous failures, and a similar situation takes place in our professional lives. If you stop reading this book right now and think about the assumptions you have made in the last week, yesterday, or as recently as today, you will quickly agree with me; assumptions are a risky approach to life in general, and wrong assumptions can simply be devastating.

You leave home in the morning assuming it will not rain, just to later wish you had brought an umbrella. Leaving for the airport with just enough time to make your flight, assuming traffic will not be a problem, just to realize your plane is already in the air while you are still miles away from the airport.

We can find literally thousands of examples in our daily lives to illustrate how our own *wrong* assumptions could lead us to individual failures of various magnitudes. Let us now see what this looks like on the business side of the pond.

When managing projects, we make assumptions regularly; from the moment we assume that the amount of time and money we have at our disposal to successfully complete the project are going to be enough, to the time we assume our customer is going to agree with our execution and deviation strategies. Time after time, we discover that the large majority of our assumptions are simply wrong, and as Brian Tracy said, wrong assumptions lead the way to big failures.

If I have to describe the one instance where wrong assumptions have the most devastating results, I would have to say it is in the world of business development and sales. I have been a sales leader for many years and have helped many companies achieve great results during my career. Inevitably, I have always observed that the single biggest mistake professionals at all levels make when pursuing business opportunities is making wrong assumptions.

During a typical tender process, we work extremely hard to prepare the best proposal possible. However, in doing so, we make a number of assumptions which have the potential of being right or wrong. A typical example is the assumption that our competitors will price their bids higher than we will, or that one bidder will not submit a quote at all, or that the customer will like our offering better than that of the competition, regardless of price.

We are surrounded by assumptions, in fact I once read an article that explained that the number one brain activity we as humans do during our lives is to make decisions; while the second brain activity in our daily lives is to make assumptions. Can you guess how many of the assumptions we make in one year are wrong? I do not know the answer to that question, and I would certainly prefer not to venture into making an assumption about it.

The truth to the matter is that our assumptions are hunting us down, chasing us every day of our personal and professional lives. Assumptions themselves are not the problem, there is nothing bad about assuming things; the problem begins when our assumptions are wrong. *"Wrong assumptions lie at the root of every failure"* (Brian Tracy).

The trick is to get in the habit of questioning our own assumptions, as a way to minimize the risk of getting undesired results based on wrong suppositions. If you stay alert, you will find opportunities to challenge assumptions virtually every day in your personal and professional lives. I can guarantee that in every meeting that you attend, the group makes assumptions and seldom do team members take the time to go back and assess what led them to a negative outcome.

You can easily implement this practice in your career, by simply questioning or challenging every assumption that attendees make during meetings. My suggestion is to make a list of assumptions during the course of every meeting, at the end of which the team should review them and agree to keep them attached to the minutes of meeting. The purpose is to document what was assumed and the possible consequences of each assumption. You can go as far as assigning a probability factor to each case, similar to the way you perform risk analysis.

I was recently part of a series of meetings to design a go-to-market strategy for one of my clients. I silently kept a log of every assumption made during the three days of discussion. At the end of the exercise, the team was happy to announce they had finished creating the market-entry strategy, which actually represented several millions of dollars in new revenues for the company.

Before concluding the last day of sessions, I presented the list of assumptions I had prepared and challenged every single one of them. The team had to visualize a situation whereby every assumption was wrong, and the results certainly looked devastating. Then we engaged in a thorough analysis of every assumption and we qualified the probability and impact of each. Some were less likely to materialize, but their impact on the result was sometimes greater than in the case of those more likely to occur.

At the end, we had a much more realistic view of the project and we could now easily visualize the effects of the newly created go-to-market strategy. By realizing we have made a significant number of assumptions along the way, and by questioning them, we were able to adjust the strategy to a more realistic playfield and a more likely outcome.

The meeting extended into an extra day, but as we later discovered, it was well worth it.

One can write a separate book on the subject of assumptions, particularly on the analysis of the devastating effects that wrong assumptions can have on the results of the modern corporation. You will be astonished to hear the number of assumptions that people make in the corporate world every day, paving the road to potentially disastrous results.

Unconventional Project Managers and Business Developers are always aware of the assumptions they are making, and they always question their own assumptions, especially when planning or strategizing. Two simple questions are the key to avoiding what I call *death by assumption*:

1. What are my assumptions?

2. Could my assumptions be wrong?

By forcing yourself and your colleagues to answer those two fundamental questions you will be creating an environment conducive to more effective plans and strategies, which inevitably will result in higher success rates.

Challenge your assumptions, and enjoy the results.

Appendix A:

Presentation and Public Speaking Tips

Public speaking and making presentations is typically a core competency of sales professionals, but more often than not project managers and subject matter experts have to present their work before audiences of all sizes. We have all been in that situation at some point in our careers; shockingly, we usually go home feeling we could have done a better job.

Why do we feel that way? Why is it so difficult to identify what it is that we could have done differently to make the presentation better for the audience? Why do we always feel that the other presenters are much better than we are at speaking in public?

There is a significant amount of material out there on this subject, and I encourage you to seek out the best books and training material on the matter, if you feel this is an area for improvement. However, I would like to offer you a few very simple tips that could help you get started:

1. Avoid *death by PowerPoint* at all costs, keeping your slideshows brief and entertaining, following these very simple rules:

-   People in the audience generally know how to read. If reading off your slides is all you are going to do, you may as well give them a copy and go home.

- The purpose of the slide is to <u>assist</u> you in <u>illustrating</u> some key points of your topic.
- Slides should be primarily graphical, avoiding text, which includes bullet points.
- Use photos, drawings, diagrams, illustrations, artwork, clipart, video, etc.
- Use engaging colors and large font. Remember, the person sitting in the back of the room must be able to see your slides too.
- If you must show a bullet-point list, do not animate each line. Show them all at once. It is annoying.

2. Slides do not need to represent everything you are going to say. Feel free to talk at length about a topic without having a supporting slide at all. There is nothing wrong with that.

3. Reject podiums. You should never agree to make a presentation from a static podium position, unless you are a politician. Always plan and make sure there will be a wireless microphone available for you to move around, or better yet, bring your own lapel microphone if you can.

4. <u>Never</u> give your back to the audience. Most amateur presenters make this mistake when reading from the slide show. You should never face the screen, and should make sure you are always facing the audience, making eye contact.

5. Never leave your laptop computer connected to the projector on the table behind you. The laptop computer should always be in front of you, so you can glance at the screen and see what the next topic is, without having to turn your back to the audience.

6. Also, under no circumstance allow another person to click the slides for you. This is another big mistake even seasoned speakers often make. You should always be in control of your show, unless you and your helper have rehearsed intensively.

7. Get yourself a good quality remote clicker, so you can click through the slides while walking and facing the audience, without having to return to your computer every time to press a button.

8. Find a good pace for your speech, never too fast, never too slow.

9. Find a good volume for your voice, never too loud, never too low.

10. Practice making your presentation without slides at all. Once you are comfortable presenting your topic without slides, then build a brief set of slides to assist you in illustrating some key points, never the other way around.

11. Know your topic, then rehearse, rehearse, and rehearse; and when you are done rehearsing, then rehearse some more.

Appendix B:

Time Management & Procrastination

People often ask me about time management tips. When I start interrogating people about their daily routine, I discover that the problem is not necessarily time, but their procrastination habits. I am a chronic procrastinator myself; I cannot avoid the temptation to do the things I enjoy the most first, sacrificing those that I do not, which are usually the most important ones.

Again, there are hundreds of books and training courses on time management if you are interested, but I thought I would share with you what has worked best, at least in my case:

First, feeling there are not enough hours in the day to do all the things we have to do is, in my opinion, a good sign. It means we are busy, which typically means we are contributing to society, our families, and ourselves. It means we are producing something. Now the question is: Are we producing efficiently? Are we maximizing our productivity? Can we improve the way we do things so that we can be productive in all fronts of our professional and personal lives?

It seems as though getting things done is our only job; we go about our lives running errands, opening correspondence, paying bills, buying groceries, taking our children to and from places, getting our hair cut, going to the doctor, the dentist, the lawyer, etc. On top of everything, we go to school and/or work, and there we live our parallel lives, full of other not less important tasks.

21st Century technology has made it possible for us to connect with others in real-time. Email, text messages, social network updates, and phone calls have invaded our lives, to the point that we find it difficult to concentrate on a single task without our *digital life* distracting us. All these elements are contributing factors to our inability to manage time.

It all boils down to prioritization and concentration. What has worked the best in my own case is to make a list of the work-related tasks I need to complete and a separate list for the personal life tasks that also need my attention. Then I sort both lists according to priorities, putting the most important activities at the top.

Once I know what needs to be done and by when, I highlight those things that could easily be delegated to others. I assigned some of the personal tasks to family members and some of the work related priorities to colleagues at work. Then I deal with the things that remain in my own "to do" lists.

I color-code each task according to my interests. Things I completely dislike go in red; those that I really enjoy go in green, and those that I am indifferent about go in yellow. Every night I make a list of the things I want/need to accomplish the next day. I put some of the red items first to get them out of the way quickly, then a few green tasks to energize my day, and I toss a few yellow ones at the end of the day.

Every day is different, some are more on the red side than others are, while others are greener, but I never let a day go by without having a combination of all three colors. More importantly, the very last activity of each day is in blue, which represents my reward. After a productive day, defined by the accomplishment of tasks in each color category, I reward myself with one activity that I really enjoy. It can be a nap, a glass of wine, a walk in the park, a movie, a date with my wife, cooking, or simply sitting outside enjoying some unwinding time in fresh air.

I do ten minutes of personal social network updates in the morning, ten minutes after lunch, and ten minutes in the evening. I never let the (personal) Internet tasks occupy more than the allotted time, otherwise my productivity declines, and I run the risk of missing my reward. I do have my business related Internet tasks, but those have a different priority over my personal social networks.

Seldom do I take or make unscheduled phone calls, but if an old friend calls after months without speaking with each other, I take the call and I use it as my reward for the day. In the end, I do not let anything affect my overall schedule.

Lastly, I never procrastinate, or at least I try to control the temptation to do so. In fact, I developed this system as a response to my own procrastination *addiction*; this is my way of saying no to deferring things for later.

I encourage you to find your own system, the one that works for you. Getting enough hours of sleep is another important tool to getting things done. If you are not getting at least seven hours of sleep per night, chances are you are not managing the "pending things" list effectively.

Appendix C:
Negotiations

A customer once asked me what my definition for negotiation was. Astonished by his question—especially because we were starting the negotiation of a multimillion-dollar contract—I came up with an answer that was as honest as it was improvised:

"Well, in my opinion a negotiation is simply the process by which two or more parties find ways to compromise on their individual positions regarding a particular issue (it could be financial or otherwise) with the purpose of finding an agreement that is somewhat satisfactory to all involved."

We have all been part of negotiations, both in our personal and professional lives. Our childhood was full of negotiation moments with our siblings and parents. Our adolescent life gave us even more exposure to this practice, as we learned new, more effective negotiation methods. Later we learned how to negotiate compensation packages, vacation weeks, promotions, and even departure deals with our employers. We also learned to compromise with our spouse and children on a daily basis, and so the cycle repeats itself.

Project Managers are in constant negotiation with their clients, as they discuss and agree to unplanned events, scope changes, and additions to the project regularly. Sometimes one party does not deliver on the contractual terms of the project and the other party seeking compensation takes legal action. Whenever litigation occurs there is always an opportunity for negotiation.

Lawyers often say, *"It is always better a bad agreement than a good lawsuit."* Those are smart words, as the cost of legal action for both parties often surpasses the outcome. A dear friend once asked me after a business meeting in Rio de Janeiro: *"Who wins during a lawsuit?"* His humoristic answer was *"Both lawyers do."*

There are many different negotiation styles; some are trans-actional-based, while others are relationship-oriented. The idea that one party needs to lose for the other to win is a misconception that has had a very negative impact on the perceived meaning of the nego-tiation exercise in general.

It all depends on how much each party values the relationship with each other. If neither party has an interest in having or main-taining a relationship with the other part, then negotiations will be hard and confrontational.

Skilled negotiators are able to clearly define the issue at hand and put it in the center of the table, away from the hands of all involved. Once everybody can clearly observe the argument from afar then it is easier to define *the goal*, or the ideal outcome that allows all parties be satisfied.

With that clear objective in mind, effective negotiators can easily convince their *opponents* that reaching an agreement that achieves *the goal* will benefit everybody, and for that reason, the smart thing to do is to brainstorm collectively on ideas to accomplish that objective.

Suddenly a cooperation spirit is born and silo walls are torn-down. The notion that one must lose in order for the other to win magically dissipates, and a team approach flourishes in search for answers that would allow the group to find the common ground needed to settle the dispute.

Negotiation styles can go from the simple *haggling* and *bar-gaining*, through the—in my opinion overrated—*win-win*, all the way to the more complex *joint problem solving* approaches. Each situa-tion is different and calls for different negotiation styles, depending on the circumstances.

Effective negotiators have mastered their ability to identify the personality and negotiation style of their counterparts quickly, so they can immediately adapt their own repertoire to maintain a leveled negotiation field.

There are numerous books and training opportunities to master the art of negotiation. It is important that we face these situations as just another aspect of our jobs. It is not about a give and take exercise to achieve a win-win scenario anymore; negotiations have turned into a very sophisticated skill that we should all practice and master in order to be successful in our careers.

Final Words

Writing this book has been as much fun as it has been challenging. I have enjoyed tremendously the exercise of organizing my thoughts and the hundreds of notes that I have taken over the years during meetings and philosophical discussions about business development, project management, sales, and the evolution of the corporate world.

The book was purposely written as a collection of essays, because I felt the need to keep things simple and to the point. I did my best in trying to keep the material at a basic level, so anyone could benefit from reading it.

In addition, I did not want this book to be *heavy* or *dry*, which would have made it boring. I wanted the book to be engaging and entertaining, fun to read, and illustrative, using simple real-life examples.

Despite its title, *The Unconventional Project Manager* is a book directed to a very broad audience. As I said in the first pages, the material is most effective when all stakeholders in the organization read and embrace the concepts covered in this book. Winning in business is a team effort and we are all called upon to help our fellow salespeople in their quest for bringing in new orders.

If at times you felt this was a sales book, it was because in essence it is. If you were diligent in reading every chapter in the book you have probably discovered that Sales is not exclusively a sales team function anymore, and now you better understand the crucial role that other professionals, especially project and service managers, can (should) play in helping the company achieve greater success in its quest for growth.

I truly hope the concepts I developed in this book help you further your career and your personal life. The only message to my audience now is not be afraid of putting the lessons of *The Unconventional Project Manager* into practice, and to challenge your company to think outside the box and implement the business development strategies I have shared in the preceding pages. The results will amaze you and will help you take your career and company to new heights.

Thank you for the time you spent going over these pages and for passing on the message of this book. I wish you lasting success and a rewarding career.

Unconventionally Yours,

George Galaz, Sr.

Credits

Apple, iPod, iPad, and iPhone are trademarks of Apple Inc., registered in the U.S. and other countries.

Sony, Walkman, and Betamax are trademarks of Sony, its parent and/or its affiliates.

Palm and HP are trademarks of Hewlett-Packard Company.

Coca-Cola is a trademark of The Coca-Cola Company.

Becoming Preferred and Michael Vickers are trademarks of Summit Learning Systems Inc.

Brian Tracy is a professional speaker and bestselling author (www.BrianTracy.com).

LinkedIn is a trademark of LinkedIn Corporation.

Twitter is a trademark of Twitter Inc.

Facebook is a trademark of Facebook, Inc.

The Art of War is a book originally written by army general Sun Tzu, more than 2,000 years ago and studied, analyzed, and re-edited by several contemporary authors and historians.

About The Author

George Galaz, Sr. is a Canadian citizen born in Chile in 1969. With a background in computer science, he started his career in the marketing and advertising services industry, quickly moving into project management roles and leading teams. He was also an instructor at Universidad de Chile's Faculty of Continuing Education.

In the early '90s, he co-founded a successful computer business that still thrives today and enjoys the reputation of being one of Chile's preferred computer and technology shops.

In Canada, he joined the energy sector as a Senior Project Manager for a technology multinational company, where he managed various complex high-tech projects for Oil & Gas customers in Africa, Europe, North, Central, and South America.

His unconventional and progressive project management style made him the first PM to receive sales commissions without being a salesperson. After about six years of successfully running international projects, he joined the sales team of this company as Director of Sales. He continued to refine his unconventional sales and customer satisfaction strategies, completely transforming the traditional approach to revenue and profit generation. George also spent time coaching fellow Project Managers on his theories and strategies, completely changing the typical role of the PM.

In 2005, he joined the Executive MBA program at the Haskayne School of Business, University of Calgary, where he studied economics, marketing, finance, international business, data modeling, business leadership, and corporate governance—among other subjects.

In 2006, he accepted a promotion in Caracas, Venezuela as Vice President and General Manager with the same company. After successful three years, he relocated to Houston, Texas in early 2009, as the company's Director of Business Development. Two years later, he decided to leave this large NASDAQ-traded company to join an even larger Fortune 500 multinational technology corporation.

During all these years, George has mastered his *Revenue-Generation* techniques that made him a very successful Project Manager and Sales leader very early in his career. In 2012, he started writing *The Unconventional Project Manager*™, the first book in its class to cover the topic of understanding and leveraging the role of Project Managers, Service, and Technical Teams in the revenue-generation process.

George is the founder of **Sales4PMs**™; an organization that provides tailored in-house and web-based Seminars and Coaching programs, designed to help corporations of all sizes reach their revenue growth and market share objectives.

George also delivers his insights and strategies in powerful Keynote presentations at trade shows, conferences, and corporate events.

www.Sales4PMs.com

author@Sales4PMs.com

24642832R60117

Made in the USA
Charleston, SC
02 December 2013